Saint Junípero Serra

8.19.2015

Jackie,

¡Siempre adelante!

Christian Clifford

Saint Junípero Serra

MAKING SENSE OF THE HISTORY AND LEGACY

Christian Clifford

Foreword by Tommy King, O.F.M., D.Min.

ISBN: 1511862297
ISBN 13: 9781511862295
Library of Congress Control Number: 2015906846
CreateSpace Independent Publishing Platform
North Charleston, South Carolina

Dedication

To my students — past, present and future. My prayer is that on your quest, you see more clearly, as Pope John Paul II put it, the splendor of truth.[1] Walt Whitman wrote in *Leaves of Grass*,
    "O truth of the earth! O truth of things! I am determined to press
                    the whole way toward you,
    Sound your voice! I scale mountains or dive in the sea after you."[2]
    Saint Serra can bring us to the depths of what Whitman shares if we open our minds and hearts to his story.

Cover Photo: Mission Dolores Basilica, San Francisco, California (Franz Mayer & Co., Munich, Germany, ca. 1926).

---

1 John Paul II, Encyclical Letter, *Veritatis splendor*, August 6, 1993, accessed February 11, 2014, http://w2.vatican.va/content/john-paul-ii/en/encyclicals/documents/hf_jp-ii_enc_06081993_veritatis-splendor.html.
2 Walt Whitman, *Leaves of Grass* (New York: Penguin Classics, 1986), 144.

Table of Contents

Foreword

In 1221, St. Francis of Assisi wrote in his Earlier Rule to his brothers who would be *Those Going Among the Saracens and Other Nonbelievers*:

> As for the brothers who go, they can live spiritually among the Saracens and nonbelievers in two ways. One way is not to engage in arguments or disputes but to be subject *to every human creature for God's sake* (1 Pt. 2:13) and to acknowledge that they are Christians. The other way is to announce the Word of God, when they see it pleases the Lord, in order that [unbelievers] may believe in almighty God, the Father, the Son and the Holy Spirit, the Creator of all, the Son, the Redeemer and Savior, and be baptized and become Christians because *no one can enter the kingdom of God without being reborn of water and the Holy Spirit* (Jn. 3:5). -*Earlier Rule,* Chapter XVI, 5-7

Junípero Serra affectionately called his fellow Franciscan missionary brothers *Padre Predicador* (Father Preacher). Inspired by the desire of St. Francis for his missionary brothers to preach in words but most importantly by their example (*Earlier Rule,* Chapter XVII, 2), I believe that same desire drove Serra some five centuries later to leave the comfort of European academic life in Mallorca to a missionary life in New Spain. That desire was to preach the Gospel of Jesus Christ to those who had never heard it.

After working for eleven years as a missionary in Guatemala and Peru, I have a much greater appreciation of Serra's missionary accomplishments than when I just heard about him when I was being educated in Catholic schools in California. In terms of "creature comforts," my life as a missionary was much easier than that of Serra. However, it is amazing how many similar struggles I had in common with Serra, even though he ministered in the eighteenth century and I in the twenty-first. We both had great difficulties communicating with other missionaries and religious superiors, dealt with loneliness and isolation, lacked materials and space to conduct catechetical and evangelization activities, had an inadequate understanding of local cultures, great distances existed between us and the people to whom we wanted to minister and, most interestingly, both of us had constant struggles with government authorities who impeded our desire to evangelize the way we felt best. It is clear to me that Serra accomplished much more in the proclamation of the Gospel than I did, under much greater difficulties that I had to deal with. It is so appropriate that he is acknowledged as a great missionary saint of the Church.

Saints are ordinary people whom the Church recognizes have lived the Gospel in extraordinary ways. As all saints, Serra sought to live and proclaim the Gospel in a particular socio-historical context. Even though we might evangelize in our own particular socio-historical context in different ways than Serra did, he sought to embrace in his life and ministry those qualities of the Gospel that are timeless – compassion, joy, mercy, service, sacrificing for the well-being of another, just to name a few.

Junípero Serra should have the title Saint because his life models living the Gospel for the rest of us. Amid a new wave of criticism against Serra for his style of evangelization, Christian Clifford shows in this work that those of us who want to faithfully live the Gospel have a lot to learn from Serra. He clearly points out that Spanish colonialism must not be confused with evangelization techniques of Serra and his brother Franciscan missionaries in New Spain in the late eighteenth century.

Christian felt it was important to provide critically thinking Christians a "popular" style book that would be easy to read and informative, and at the same time to help people of faith see both the holiness and humanity of Serra. I believe he has hit the mark. The author blends his love for the study of history, his theological training and his enthusiasm for the proclamation of the Gospel to help us be inspired by Serra the man, the eighteenth century missionary and the saint. The author guides the reader through a process of explaining the valid historical method he used to look honestly at Serra's life and accomplishments, helpful historical information about Serra as a Spanish Franciscan missionary in New Spain, selected primary sources of Serra's own writings, and explanation of the process of canonizing a saint and, most importantly, what Junípero Serra has to teach us Christians of the twenty-first century about effectively living and proclaiming the Gospel. This is a simple book, but the reader can be assured of Christian's study and use of solid contemporary scholarship about Serra in its composition.

Christian envisions this book as a helpful tool for high school religion classes to study this new saint of the Church. However, I see this book as a helpful resource for people of faith of all ages to see the blessings of Serra's witness to the Gospel life and what he can teach us today about effective evangelization. The Church has made Junípero Serra a saint because his life and words have much to teach about being faithful Christians. This book is a wonderful guide to help us enter into this process.

Tommy King, O.F.M., D.Min.
Pastor
St. Boniface Church
San Francisco, California

C H A P T E R   1

Do We Know What Serra Looked Like?

We do not know exactly what Junípero Serra looked like. Based on the description of Serra before setting sail for New Spain in the Spanish government's Board of Trade in Cádiz, we know that Serra was "a lector of theology, native of Petra in the Diocese of Mallorca, thirty-five years old, of medium height, swarthy, dark eyes and hair, scant beard"[3] (What "medium height" meant was cleared up when Serra's remains were exhumed in 1943 for the canonization process: he stood five feet, two inches tall). The **Franciscan** Friars of the Province of Santa Barbara web site adds: "He had a sonorous voice, had swarthy skin, dark hair and eyes."[4] Within a year after his death a painting

Inset of Guerrero piece.

Source: Maynard Geiger, *Father Junípero Serra Paintings*, 10.

was commissioned in New Spain, and his fellow Mallorcan, missionary **priest**, friend, and biographer — Francisco Palóu (1723-1789) — eventually saw it. The likeness, painted in 1785 by Marianus Guerrero for

---

3 Gregory Orfalea, *Journey to the Sun: Junípero Serra's Dream and the Founding of California* (New York: Scribner, 2014), 62.

4 "Blessed Junipero Serra," *Franciscan Friars of the Province of Santa Barbara*, accessed February 11, 2015, https://sbfranciscans.org/about/blessed-junipero-serra.

the College of San Fernando and titled — *Verdado Retrato del Aposólico Padre Predicador Fr. Junípero Serra Natural de la Villa Petra en el Reino de Mallorca* — is one of the closest images we have in space and time to the actual man. However, is it really that important to know how the man looked? Or is it more important to know who the man was — his heart and works being the greatest measure of his character and accomplishments? Palóu summed up his great friend best in his biography of Serra, *Relación histórica*, published in 1787, "His memory shall not fail, because the works he performed when alive shall be impressed in the minds of the dwellers of this New California."[5]

---

5 General Notes:
First, during Serra's time, Alta (or Upper) California was known as New (Nueva) California and Baja (or Lower) California was known as Old (Antigua) California. The designations Alta and Baja began in 1804. See Map in Appendix.
Next, the terms Native American, Indian, and American Indian are still commonly used and accepted, but more often the Native uses his or her specific tribal name. No references have been changed when using direct quotes. I selected to use the reference Native or Native American, depending on the context.
Also, a Glossary of the words and terms in **bold** has been provided for the reader's benefit. All definitions are from Wikipedia.org or Merriam-Webster.com, unless noted otherwise.
Last, all scripture references are from the New American Bible Revised Edition.

CHAPTER 2

The Quest

To understand Serra, one has to understand the people he set out to serve, the Native population of North America. I had to discover Serra gradually over time in several steps.

My quest began unexpectedly when I found myself attracted to the story of the Native peoples of the Americas. That was in 1995 when I was twenty-four years old and living in Great Falls, Montana. Unlike my native San Francisco Bay Area where the descendants of the historic Natives seem invisible, they are quite present in Montana. For example, at the University of Great Falls I took the class Culture and Traditions of Montana Native Americans, taught by professor Clayton Quiver, and developed a personal perspective and gained insight into the culture and traditions of Native Americans. My general knowledge of Native American history was limited to what I had learned in 4th grade and

Clifford Beck (1946-1995),
Winds of Change, lithograph

in high school United States History class about the California missions and the mistreatment and injustice done to Natives by the United States government. Though my knowledge was limited, I was somehow drawn to the Natives' story of perseverance, probably because I saw a correlation with the story of the Irish under British rule, a fascination of mine because of my ethnic background. Thanks to my professor, a Lakota Sioux, I did come away from the class with a new appreciation for Native Americans.

For a week in 2003, I had the opportunity, with a service group of high school students, to visit the Navajo Reservation in northeastern Arizona. We helped with demolition work, built a shed, painted, and assisted with sheepherding duties. We visited the Navajo Nation government offices in Window Rock and Saint Michael Indian School, the latter financed by heiress turned religious Katherine Drexel and opened in 1902. The highlight was Easter Mass at Our Lady of Fatima Parish in Chinle. The church was packed and the group I was with were the only non-Natives there. I saw the diversity of the Church and the Resurrection in a profound way. Despite the constant issues of alcoholism, drug abuse, unemployment, and criminal activity on the Navajo Nation, I was able to see a powerful light amidst the darkness.

The next step on my quest was when I began teaching at Serra High School in San Mateo, California. Who really was the school's namesake? Therefore, I visited all twenty-one missions over a few summers while on road trips to visit friends. I developed a new appreciation for the missions, especially for its first father president (priest and administrator), Junípero Serra. I had read so much about the little friar from Mallorca, I considered him one of my closest friends. I was stunned to discover that not everyone saw Serra in a positive light.

In 2012 I received a copy of *Mission Labor* by Bill Morgan, a retired elementary teacher in San Francisco Public Schools. It was written for fourth grade public school students. I read it and was shocked, to say the least. The author provided little evidence to support the many black-and-white claims he made. It seemed to me he was using history as a weapon to support his own ideology. The illustrations were disturbing: happy Natives, followed by intrusive Spaniards with fleeing Natives, and then Natives being marched by a lance-wielding Spaniard at a mission. This portrayal of a utopia before Europeans came was fantasy. I was thankful that *Mission Labor* is not a mandatory part of the curriculum.

I wrote to the author about my concerns and he responded that his work "was meant to provide a counter voice to the literally hundreds of books for children that are, either directly or by implication, pro-missionary and either ignore completely or pass over the Indian point of view." He went on, "This is the purpose of this book — to present the history of California from the point of view of the people who did the work — in this case, the Native Americans." To my point in my email on the encyclical of Pope Paul III *Sublimus Dei* (*The Sublime God*), written in 1537, stating that slavery and abuse of native peoples was contradictory to Catholic faith, he flippantly retorted, "It's nice that the Pope consid-ered mistreatment 'contradictory to the Catholic faith,' but as anyone on the streetcorner [sic] could tell you, the Pope was in Rome and the natives (and their maltreaters) were in California." To have any child walk away thinking that life for the Natives in California was like that of the American slave was blatantly dishonest as has been exposed time and again by the scholarly community. Bill Morgan's response to this was; "I think it's clear that for many Indians, mission life was, if not enslavement, then forced labor." That was a bold statement for Morgan to make, but I was unconvinced from my own experience that someone like Morgan had an unbiased perspective to talk for the descendants of the Mission Indians. I suspected he was making a claim to speak for them when he was only using them as a prop for making his own pronouncement.

On April 24, 2014, I walked the Devil's Slide Trail in Pacifica, California, a segment of the old Highway 1 that gives hikers, runners, bi-cyclists and equestrians amazing views of the Pacific Ocean. I was dumb-struck, this time by certain language used on the Interpretive Sign titled *On the Trail of History.*

The County of San Mateo Parks sign states that in the Spanish Colonial Period section for the year 1776, "Missions use newly baptized natives as captive labor." The author went on to state the work done by native men and women and refers to this work as "hard labor." The language used — "captive labor" and "hard labor" — is misleading.

When I returned to school, I asked my eleventh grade high school students what they thought when they heard the terms "captive labor" and "hard labor." They answered in unison, "slavery!" I had to do something, so I contacted the county agency and informed them that use of such language is inaccurate and demanded it be stricken and changed to reflect the general consensus of mission scholars.

When I spoke with my classes in January 2015 about Pope Francis' announcement of Serra's canonization, the reaction was one of general excitement. The predominant question was if the school would change its name to *Saint* Serra High School. Soon after, I taught the historical method and its practicality, bringing up my challenge to the choice of language on the sign at Devil's Slide, of "captive labor" and "hard labor" conjuring images of slavery in the Antebellum South. I was met with questions such as, "Well, was it?" Another student emailed, "I wanted to look more in depth about what you said about the mission system, so I found a few articles that were worth knowing. I just wanted to know what you thought about the article. I looked into the author, and he is a man who has published books and various articles on the topic. He got his resources from various primary source letters and books from UC Berkeley. Just wanted to know what you thought about the article." The author in question had the word "enslavement" in his book's title. Another young man who read in a book that the Catholic monks of the Middle Ages introduced new crops, industries, and production methods asked, "If the book shows and tells that the monks were helpful everywhere they went, how come there are always stories that the monks of the monasteries used the people as slaves and held them and forced them to work?" The treatise you hold was born out of this thirst for clarity.

The examples I have shared pertain to the California Missions. The mission story is that of Junípero Serra. You cannot have one without the other. He was the "captain of that ship." I hope to help the reader become more familiar with this great Catholic Christian Hispanic man who lived in a very different time. I am confident that Serra lived the Catholic understanding of a saint. Those who condemn him outright revile the life of an innocent man. He "practiced heroic virtue and lived in fidelity to God's grace"[6] in an imperfect world. Or, to borrow Michael Paul Gallagher's paraphrase of the opening paragraph of *Guadium et Spes*, "Our highest human goal is to encounter God. We are born from love, kept alive by love, and fullness of life comes when we recognize this love and freely embrace it."[7] Serra wanted nothing more than to be this love for others. Getting to the truth, though, is not easy.

One thing is certain, however — you deserve the truth. I hope that my sharing my personal quest to know Junípero Serra will help you in your search.

---

6 *Catechism of the Catholic Church*, 2nd ed (Vatican City: Libreria Editrice Vaticana, 2000), 828.

7 Michael P. Gallagher, *Faith Maps: Ten Religious Explorers from Newman to Joseph Ratzinger* (New York: Paulist Press, 2010), 5.

CHAPTER 3

The Search for Truth and the Historical Method

"Seek truth while you are young, for if you do
not, it will later escape your grasp."
Plato, (5th-4th c. BC), *Parmenides*[8]
"O sweet light of my hidden eyes . . . there are three
times . . . present of things past, memory;
present of things present, sight; present
of things future, expectation."
St. Augustine of Hippo (A.D. 354-430), *Confessions*, Book XI[9]

One of the many benefits of studying history is that it helps make sense of the complex. Like a detective, the **historian** has tools to help sift through the many voices and come to a solid conclusion that has a high degree of certainty. It is called the *historical method*.

This is a story of doing just that. When news broke on January 15, 2015, of Pope Francis' announcement that during his September visit to the United States he would canonize Junípero Serra, I did a Google Alert (a monitoring of the web for interesting new content). I simply went to Google Alert and typed in the words "Junípero Serra canonization." Daily I received in my inbox all new Web sources that pertained to the search string. Most articles in the press and blogosphere painted

---

8 "The Pope and Plato." *L'Osservatore Romano*. August 20, 2011, accessed February 23, 2015, http://www.osservatoreromano.va/en/news/the-pope-and-plato.
9 Augustine, *Confessions*. (San Bernardino, CA: Benton Press, 2013), 157.

Serra in a negative light. Words such as *enslaver, genocidal, forceful, exploiter, sadistic, brutal,* and *intolerant* were thrown around like dirty laundry. I knew otherwise. Most harsh accusations made against Serra were unsubstantiated claims. It was a somber reminder that one can write and say anything.

The following list is not exhaustive, but what is included are the basic steps that all historians take.

1. The historian asks questions born out of interest. It takes a lot of work to find a substantive answer, but the reward will be great. This passion enables one to put in the hard work, just like the greatest athletes.
2. The historian needs a foundation of knowledge based on the following questions;

* Who is present?
* When did the event take place?
* How did the event happen?
* What took place?
* Where did it happen?
* Why did it happen?

Answers to these basic questions form the framework for one's research and provides context for the big question one wants to answer substantively. For example, let us say one has a friend of another religion. He wants to know what his religion has in common with his friend's. One needs to have the basic knowledge of the two religions in order to trace origins and relationships and raise meaningful questions.

3. Identify and evaluate sources
    a. Gather multiple sources. Some questions to ask that will help you decide if the source is valid or not are the following;

Who is the author? What makes them experts on the subject? What are their points of view? Is it current or dated material? Or are both needed?

    b. Read and analyze the evidence. Does the author make sound generalizations? What assumptions (an accepted truth, without proof) does he or she make?

    c. *Ad fontes!* To the source! Primary sources (firsthand accounts) are a must. Do not rely only on information from those who were not at the events (secondary sources). In regard to secondary sources, ask if they make sound arguments with sufficient evidence.

4. Interpret the past

    a. How has the research changed the answer you had before you started? Did you change or add to your previous understanding? How did this help you make more sense out of the complex topic?

5. Refrain from making questionable judgments

    a. Always be aware of them. Practice empathy, not presentism. Empathy is when we put ourselves in the shoes of those in the past. Empathy does not excuse past actions, but helps us at least understand another perspective. This may shed lights on one's own. Presentism is when we project our current norms and values onto the past. When one sees the past only through this lens, one becomes limited from what can be gained from studying the past.

The Christian uses the historical method, too. However, we are called to see history in a unique way. We know what Saint Augustine meant when he wrote in his biography *Confessions*, ". . . present of things future, expectation." It is no surprise that we use the phrases *before Christ* and *anno Domini* (*in the year of our Lord*) when looking at space and time. The Incarnation is the pinnacle, or high point, of Salvation history. The ultimate meaning is comprehended by the eye of faith. Leo Cardinal Scheffczyk (1920-2005) put it this way; "The ultimate significance of studying the history of the religion of Christ is to have a 'firmer grounding of the Faith.'"[10] In other words, our questions come from a place of faith and the answers we discover deepen it.

My favorite description of Church history is from a surprising person, Marc Bloch (1886-1944). Bloch was a French historian and in the Resistance during World War II. The Gestapo captured, tortured, and executed him. He said,

> Christianity is a religion of historians . . . For sacred books, the Christians have books of history, and their liturgies commemorate, together, with episodes from the terrestrial life of God, the annals of the church and the lives of the saints. Christianity is historical in another, perhaps, even deeper sense. . . The destiny of humankind, placed between the Fall and the Judgment, appears to its eyes as a long adventure, of which each life, each individual pilgrimage, is in its turn a reflection. It is in time and, therefore, in history that the great drama of Sin and Redemption, the central axis of all Christian thought, is unfolded."[11]

Bloch reminds us that historical truth matters to the overall truth claims made by the Catholic Church.

The study of history "requires following and evaluating arguments and arriving at usable, even if tentative, conclusions based on the available evidence."[12] In other words, as we go along in life we add to our understanding, always getting us closer to the truth. If Bloch, a secular Jew,

---

10 Hubert Jedin, ed. *Handbook of Church History*, Vol. 1, "General Introduction to Church History," (Montreal: Palm Publishers, 1965), 34.

11 Marc Bloch, *The Historian's Craft* (Manchester, England: Manchester University Press, 2004), 4.

12 *California State Board of Education, History--Social Science Standards for California Public Schools*, "Historical Analysis and Interpretations" (Sacramento, CA: California Department of Education, 2000) 40-41.

can really get how Christians are called to perceive history, then there must be something to the claim that faith and reason work together to help one recognize the mystery of God in the here and now.

CHAPTER 4

The Big Picture: What I Learned
about Serra's World

It is imperative to have an understanding of the world in which the historical figure lived in order for the student of history to see through their eyes. Though limited in scope, it gives one the ability to test assumptions and practice empathy. It creates a framework to base questions on. It helps us practice humility, recognizing that the world has not always been the way one may see it today. In short, having context provides a map for the quest.

For Junípero Serra and the **society** he lived in, life was vastly different from life in today's world. He lived in the Kingdom of Spain, which was part of a much larger enterprise called Latin Christendom. When it came to religion it was, for the most part, homogeneous. The Great Commission of Jesus,[13] to spread his gospel message to all, permeated whole societies, Spain being just one. Outward signs of piety, or public religious acts, were the norm. Spain was agrarian and commercial. Disease and famine were major problems. For example, Steven Hackel, professor of History at the University of California Riverside, stated in his recent book on Serra that 25% of Mallorcans died in the epidemic of 1652.[14] The past had a huge impact on how Serra saw the part of the world he lived in.

---

13 Note: cf. Mt 28:18-22; Mk 16:15-18; Lk 24:44-49; Jn 20:19-23.
14 Steven W. Hackel, *Junípero Serra: California's Founding Father* (New York: Hill and Wang, 2013), 8.

The fifteenth century was known as the Age of Exploration or Discovery. Because of the new and exotic phenomena found abroad (particularly spices), demand for them rose. Colonizers followed the explorers to the new lands and needed laborers. As colonization spread, eighteenth century Christendom would experience (and be challenged by) the Age of Enlightenment, which advocated that reason was the primary source for legitimacy and authority. Medical journalist Sharon Basaraba estimates life expectancy "hovered between the ages of 30 and 40."[15] In Serra's world the tallest buildings were cathedrals. Although Spaniards had been present in New Spain in some capacity for roughly 250 years, Serra found a world different from the one he knew when he set foot on Veracruz on December 17, 1749.

A look at the events taking place before Junípero Serra's time will help one to see the world as he saw it. In 1492, Christopher Columbus sailed to what he thought was Asia. He hoped to meet and convert the Great Khan, who expressed interest in Christianity, and be granted trading rights for his financiers, King Ferdinand of Aragon and Queen Isabella of Castille. According to Carol Delaney, a cultural **anthropologist** and long-time professor at Stanford University, the coffers would be used to pay for a crusade to take Jerusalem back from the Muslims. In the Spaniard mind, Jesus would return soon in all His glory to Christian lands, triumphant after one

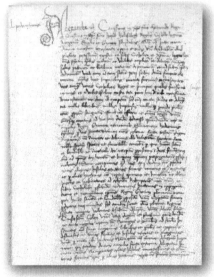

The Bull *Inter caetera* of Alexander VI addressed to the Spanish Monarchs following the Discovery of the New World, Rome, May 4, 1493.

---

15 Sharon Basaraba. "Longevity Throughout History: How has human life expectancy changed over time?" *About.com.* December 16, 2014, accessed February 4, 2015, http://longevity.about.com/od/longevitystatsandnumbers/a/Longevity-Throughout-History.htm.

last battle with evil powers. Therefore, Jerusalem, the place where Jesus' passion, death, and resurrection took place, had to be in Christian hands. Instead, Columbus landed in what is now Haiti. The Spanish elite responded to his description of "Haiti" with great interest.[16] A rush was on to make a claim in the name of the King and Queen of Spain on these new lands.

On May 4, 1493, after some diplomacy and editing of an initial document, fellow Spaniard Pope Alexander VI issued the Papal **Bull** *Inter caetera (Among Others)*, in essence granting the monarchs the newly discovered lands. The final bull split the map in two, half for Spain and the other for Portugal. The monarchs desired papal permission due to their belief that the pope was universal sovereign. Furthermore, the Pope was excited at the prospect of carrying out Jesus' Great Commission, the sharing of Jesus' gospel to the four corners of the earth. This relationship between Church and state can clearly be seen when in 1494 Pope Alexander VI bestowed on Ferdinand and Isabella the title of *Catholic King and Queen*. Barbara Frale, a historian at the Vatican Secret Archives, reflects on the effect of *Inter cetera*: "The great hopes which had given rise to the expedition were themselves to become the source of many terrible abuses. The various expeditions went in quest for gold and forced-labour and very quickly reduced the native populations to the conditions of slavery."[17]

Between May 26 and August 13, 1521, Hernán Cortés and his new native allies, the Tlaxcallans, laid siege and captured Tenochtitlán, the capital of the Aztec Empire. Spain's new allies were bitter enemies of the Aztec.

On May 29, 1537, Pope Paul III issued *Sublimus Dei (From God on High)*, stating that slavery and abuse of native peoples was contradictory to the Roman Catholic faith.

---

16 Alton Pelowski, "Why Columbus Sailed", *Columbia*, May 24, 2014, accessed February 4, 2015, http://www.kofc.org/en/columbia/detail/2012_06_columbus_interview.html.
17 *The Vatican Secret Archives* (Antwerp, Belgium: VdH Books, 2009), 105.

At the Council of Valladolid in Spain (1550-1551), the Bishop of Chiapas (New Spain), Bartolomé de Las Casas, and humanist scholar Juan Ginés de Sepúlveda debated the use of native labor. Las Casas, a reformed slaver, argued against and Sepúlveda in favor.

Spain and England were at war from 1585-1604. One of its greatest legacies was the propaganda churned out by English Protestant Christians, known today as the **Black Legend**. Spanish Roman Catholic Christians believed that Protestants were outside the one, holy, catholic, and apostolic Church, and felt the same about Catholics. For example, Puritan preacher Andrew Willet wrote in *Hexapla* in 1620, "A forme of doctrine may be set downe by hereticall and false teachings prescribed by the Romanists to the Indians, who in their first conversion to Christianity drinke in their [Catholic] drugges and errors of doctrine."[18] The smearing of Spanish Catholic colonialism such as this left its mark, persisting in some form to this day.

The race continued between Christian powers to claim lands for new wealth and prestige. The Spanish would explore the coast of what is now California. On December 18, 1602, the Vizcaíno Expedition celebrated the first Mass in California at Monterey.

By the late seventeenth century, New Spain was well established, with more lands yet to be explored. The **encomienda** system, controlled by Roman Catholic landowners (businessmen), often turned a blind eye to Church teachings and treated the native labor force brutally. Though the missions had their flaws, they were often places of sanctuary from the most destructive forces of the Spanish presence. By the end of the seventeenth century, the encomienda system was coming to an end, eventually abolished in 1720.

In 1697, the Pious Fund of the Californias began. It was in vogue for the deeply religious and wealthy lay person in Spain and Mexico to donate money for the propagation, or sharing, of the Roman Catholic

---

18 Andrew Willet, *Hexapla*, (Cambridge: Cantrell Legge, 1620), 298, accessed April 30, 2015,
http://rarebooks.dts.edu/viewbook.aspx?bookid=1423.

faith in territory that had not been **evangelized**. It would be taken over in 1768 by King Charles III, who desired nothing more than to exert state control over the Church and her activities. Serra and the mission enterprise in New California would be recipients of the fund; however, often times Serra would have to plead with government authorities for aid.

In conclusion, compared to today an early death was almost certain and the person looked to eternity with great earnestness. The patronage system (known as *patronata real*) was something that would not be tolerated today. The monarchs made major Church appointments, thus having major influence. This was done legally through agreements and treaties with the Holy See. It resulted in a synthesis of business, politics, and religion. During my quest I was most assured that this is the world that Serra found himself.

CHAPTER 5

Serra In Spain, New Spain, Old and New California

The following is the common narrative of the life of Junípero Serra. Every quest must have a foundation of facts to build upon.

The baptism record from Petra, Mallorca, Spain, for "Miguel Joseph Serre, son of Antoni and Margarita Ferrer, a married couple," is dated November 24, 1713. Miguel grew up in a hard working family who made a meager but honest living off the land. At school, his Franciscan friar teachers noted his deep faith and natural abilities in academics. Francisco Palóu wrote of his great friend, "At an early age Junipero was well instructed by his parents in the rudiments of the holy Catholic faith; they took care to take him to hear mass at the convent church of St. Bernardino where the Franciscan fathers resided. At the convent he learned among other things, Latin and Gregorian chant. From his attention to his studies, and

Fig. 1 España Correos, 1984.

Fig. 2 España Correos, commemorating the 300th anniversary of Serra's birth, 2014.

still more from his piety and docility, the parents of Junipero concluded that God had blessed their son with a vocation to the priesthood."[19] In early January of 1730 his first application to the order would be rejected. His second try was a success. Beginning his studies in September and taking his initial vow to become a Franciscan in 1731, he studied at Lullian University in Palma from 1731 until 1737. His given name, Miguel Jose, made way for the adopted name of Junípero, after Brother Juniper, a companion and ardent disciple of St. Francis of Assisi, founder of the Franciscan Order. Ordained a priest in 1737, Serra would remain at Lullian as a philosophy professor from 1740 until 1749, living a secure life, close to his family and popular with his students.

Something persistently gnawed at him, though. At the age of thirty-six, Father Serra turned his back on the comfort and routine of academic life to answer a call for missionaries in New Spain. This call would separate him from his family, knowing full well that he would never see them face-to-face again in this life. In August 1749, accompanied by two of his university students — Fathers Francisco Palóu and Juan Crespi — he set sail for New Spain.

NEW SPAIN

Arriving in Veracruz on December 17, he set out on foot for Mexico City, site of the College of San Fernando, the hub of Franciscan activities in New Spain. It was during this arduous trek, covering more than 260 miles, that Father Serra received a taste of what lay ahead of him for the rest of his life. Early on, his left foot and leg

M. Guerrero, Correos de México, 1969.

19 Francisco Palóu, *Life of Venerable Father Junipero Serra: The First Apostle of California*, Translated by J. Adam (San Francisco: P.E. Dougherty & Co., 1884), 1-2.

became infected from an insect bite, leaving him lame and causing him pain and suffering off and on for the rest of his life. Another difficulty set in about midway on his journey. Late at night, in the middle of nowhere and believing he and his fellow traveler were going to die, a man brought them to the safety of his humble home. The man was nowhere to be found the next day. When they reached a town and inquired of the man, nobody seemed to know who they were talking about. Serra believed he had been saved by Saint Joseph!

This short, stout man, who in his prime years left home to bring a new vision of love to total strangers, ended up living among those who already knew Christ. During this time he learned at the Franciscan College of San Fernando about the natives he would serve. At a later date he acted as father president of the already established missions in the Sierra Gorda region, mainly living in the city of Jalpan (located in the north of the current state of Querétaro, Mexico). The Church there was in a state of abandonment. Serra and his confrères had to re-evangelize the people. Also while in the Sierra Gorda, he acted as a Church lawyer, arguing a major case in 1766 for the **Inquisition**. He would also go on a preaching circuit between 1758 and 1767. It was not until after around twenty years in New Spain that he would finally fulfill his wish to preach the gospel in unknown lands.

OLD CALIFORNIA, NEW SPAIN

The Roman Catholic order of priests and brothers the Society of Jesus (popularly known as the Jesuits) had been evangelizing in Old California since 1697. The order's headquarters was in Loreto. Jesuits became the supreme temporal and spiritual authority of this inhospitable land. They possessed the land by occupying it, since no land grants were given by the crown. All the products of native labor at the missions were divided among the people. However, the Jesuits did not want colonists, fearing they would disrupt the missions and their work.[20] This was the Jesuit way and made some influential people who wanted colonists jealous. Also, the Jesuits were only held accountable by their superior in Rome whose direct boss was the Pope. They were outside the patronage system. This was the backdrop for why the Pope recalled to Europe the Jesuits in Spanish "possessions" in consultation with the realm. Old California would be the last area in New Spain where the Jesuits would be suppressed, literally happening on one day — February 3, 1768. The Franciscans would take the Jesuits place in Old California, and Serra would be the father president there for a year.

Serra was to report back to José de Galvez, Visitor General of New Spain, the master planner of all things expeditionary and colonial, on the status of the peninsula. The government had reason to want colonists there. It desired a substantial port as a way station for the Manila galleons loaded with trading goods from Spain's colony, the Philippines. On September 24, 1768, the decree was made calling for colonists. Serra was outspoken against Gálvez's plans because the lands were especially inhospitable for colonization due to the scarcity of water. The colonization plan continued, but was destined for failure. Albert Greenstein of *The Historical Society of Southern California* wrote,

> The call came unexpectedly in 1769, when he [Serra] was instructed to join dragoon captain Gaspar de Portolá on an expedition to New California (what is today the state of California. Old California was then the Baja peninsula [see Map in Appendix]). The plan was to establish missions at three strategic points -- San Diego, the Monterey Bay area, and the Santa Barbara Channel area — each with a presidio or garrison for protection. Although small in size,

---

20 David Piñera Ramírez, Translated by Anita Alvarez de Williams, "The Beginning of Secular Colonization in Baja California," *The Journal of San Diego History* 23, no. 1, Winter 1977, accessed February 4, 2015, http://www.sandiegohistory.org/journal/77winter/secular.htm.

these outposts would represent Spain's claim to the region if challenged by England, Russia or another imperial power."[21]

What would be known as the Sacred Expedition would leave Loreto by land on March 28 and reach San Diego Bay on July 1, 1769. On the way, Serra established the Mission San Fernando Rey de España de Velicatá on May 14 (the only Franciscan mission in all of Old California, later transferred to the Dominicans, and abandoned in 1818). Another group would leave by land and another by sea. Supposedly during this arduous journey Serra never complained. When others noticed his pain and tried to come to his aid, he responded, "But even though I die on the road, I will not turn back."[22] It is difficult to verify that he actually said this because it was recorded by Palóu, who was not present. However, it does remind us of Serra's persistence, an attribute nearly all those who knew him acknowledged, and that that the journey from Loreto to San Diego was extremely difficult.

NEW CALIFORNIA

San Mateo County (California) Historical Association President Mitchell P. Postel presents the Spanish crown's intent for New California. "When Spain finally got around to planning for the colonization, it did so after 277 years of experience in the New World. The Spanish crown wished to live down a dark legacy that had followed Spain from the West Indies, to Mexico, to South

US Postal Service, 1985.

---

21 Albert Greenstein, "Fr. Junípero Serra," *The Historical Society of Southern California*, 1999, accessed February 6, 2015, http://www.socalhistory.org/biographies/fr-junipero-serra.html.

22 Richard F. Pourade, *The Explorers*, "Expeditions by Land," (San Diego: The Union-Tribune Publishing Company, 1960), http://www.sandiegohistory.org/books/pourade/explorers/explorerschapter9.htm.

America — one in which native peoples were ruthlessly conquered and then enslaved . . . Spain wished for itself a new image — one that had the best interests of the native people in mind. Led by Padre Junipero Serra, the vision was one of gifting a utopian Christian community to the California Indians."[23]

Can a utopia exist? Can a heaven on earth be created? My quest has given me the confidence to say emphatically that Serra came to California first and foremost to spread God's message by planting seeds of faith, though he knew of the many challenges. Jesus did teach, "The kingdom of heaven is like a mustard seed that a person took and sowed in a field. It is the smallest of all the seeds, yet when full-grown it is the largest of plants. It becomes a large bush, and the 'birds of the sky come and dwell in its branches'" (Mt 13:31-32). He was up for the task of bringing the Catholic Spanish vision to those he met.

Greenstein adds about the Sacred Expedition, "Twenty-four men aboard one of the vessels [two ships, San Carlos and San Antonio left Old California by sea] died of scurvy or plague, while many others arrived sick and disabled. Most of the Indians who had joined the two land parties

Post Vaticane,
Vatican City, 1992.

died or deserted. A relief ship carrying food and supplies from Baja was lost at sea. Father Serra, a member of the second land party [led by Portolá], limped into San Diego suffering greatly from his swollen leg. Nevertheless, on July 16, 1769, sixteen days after his arrival, he founded the first of the twenty-one California Missions, San Diego de Alcala" (see Map in Appendix). Portolá and a small group would go in search of Monterey Bay. While on this trip, the first Christian baptism

---

23 Mitchell P. Postel, "Historic Resource Study for Golden Gate National Recreation Area in San Mateo County," National Park Service U.S. Department of the Interior, 2010, accessed June 17, 2014, http://www.nps.gov/goga/historyculture/upload/San-Mateo-HRS-Introduction.pdf, 10.

in present-day California took place. On July 22, 1769, Father Francisco Gomez baptized two dying girls on the present-day Marine Corps Base Camp Pendleton near San Clemente. Serra would record his first baptism (five–year-old native Bernardino de Jesus) at Monterey on December 26, 1770. Bernardino would be present at Serra's funeral in 1784.

Amidst so many setbacks at San Diego, Portolá was ready to call it quits. Death lingered in the air, the natives were hostile (Serra consoled in his arms a dying friend after an earlier attack on the encampment), and supplies were running out. If help did not come by March 19, the feast of Saint Joseph, the expedition would have to return to Old California. Serra needed a miracle. A High Mass was said the morning of the feast day, and just before sunset their prayers were answered — a supply ship arrived. Greenstein continues; "The second Mission, San Carlos Borromeo, opened temporarily at Monterey, then permanently beside the Carmel River in 1771. Thereafter it became the headquarters of Mission operations in the state [California]."

On March 13, 1773, Serra wrote from Carmel to **Viceroy** Antonio María de Bucareli y Ursúa in Mexico City of his concerns about the military and its power. Shortly after, he travelled to Mexico City with the young **neophyte** Juan Evangelista, who must have marveled at the megalopolis of approximately 150,000. After the initial meeting with the Viceroy, Serra was asked to write a detailed list of his grievances, called the *Representación*. It had thirty-two articles, or points of contention. His primary concerns dealt with the troops and their egregious behavior (against native neophyte women in particular) due to the poor leadership of Pedro Fages, second Lieutenant Governor of New California. Bucareli ruled in Father Serra's favor on thirty of the thirty-two charges brought against Fages, and removed him from office in 1774. From beginning to end, the entire trip to secure what would be coined the bill of rights for natives in New California took roughly a year.

In 1775, a group of 600 to 800 natives attacked Mission San Diego. Father Luis Jayme and two other Spaniards would be killed, the priest becoming the first martyr in New California. Serra would ask for leniency for the murderers. Before the Sacred Expedition got underway Serra wrote to Bucareli, reminding him, "One of the most important requests I made . . . was that if the Indians, pagan or Christian, should kill me then they should be forgiven."[24]

San Buenaventura, built in 1782, was the last of the nine missions to be erected during Father Serra's tenure as the father president of the New California missions.

Serra would put his teaching skills to work, personally baptizing 98% of adult converts at Mission San Carlos Borromeo. He would travel an estimated 4,000 miles in what is now California during his personal quest, despite an often ulcerated leg.

Eleven more missions would be founded under Spain, and the last under Mexico (Mission San Francisco Solano in Sonoma, founded in 1823).

---

24 Junípero Serra, *Writings of Junípero Serra*, ed. Antonine Tibesar (Washington, D.C.: Academy of American Franciscan History, 1955), II: 405.

CHAPTER 6

In Serra's Own Words: Selected Primary Sources

Robert Galgano, Department of History, University of Richmond, wrote a book review in 2006 of Steven W. Hackel's *Children of Coyote*, on H-Net (Humanities & Social Sciences Online, an interdisciplinary forum for scholars). In the introduction he succinctly summarizes the challenge to Serra scholarship. "Despite waves of recent scholarship about Indian-Spanish relations in the Americas, many outside the field cling to **ste-reotypes** about blood-thirsty conquistadors, lascivious missionaries, and noble but benighted savages. In California history, erasing stereotypes is complicated by the debate over the possible canonization of the head of the Franciscan missions, Junípero Serra."[25] Rose Marie Beebe and Robert M. Senkewicz, professors of Spanish and History, respectively, at Santa Clara University (located on the site of the eighth California mission), write of Serra in their collection of first-person accounts, *Lands of Promise and Despair,*

> Serra was a mix of light and darkness; he was a man of great vision and great blindness, of immense zeal and immense stub-bornness. In his own mind, his goals justified his treatment of the Indians, whom he loved as the children he did not have and whom he disciplined with the same ardor with which he

---

25 Robert Galgano. Review of Steven W. Hackel. *Children of Coyote, Missionaries of Saint Francis: Indian-Spanish Relations in Colonial California, 1769-1850,* H-Net Reviews. July, 2006, accessed February 14, 2015, http://www.h-net.org/reviews/showrev.php?id=11965.

disciplined himself. His vision, like that of many of his eighteenth century contemporaries, demanded intolerance against those with different ideas about this world and the next. These qualities do not make him an angel or a devil; they simply make him a man of his time and place. His time and place were, like ours, far from perfect."[26]

How does one make sense out of these conflicting interpretations?

It can easily be argued that Serra is the most studied man in California history. He left many records. Much of Serra's own words are now accessible online. The largest collection of items related to Serra, known as Serrana, can be found at the Santa Bárbara Mission Archive Library.[27]

Primary sources are key to any sound examination. Like no other, the following give us a glimpse of the man. They act as beacons of truth in the sometimes confusing sea of disambiguation surrounding the legacy of Junípero Serra. Though selective, they do cover the breadth of his life.

Cadíz, Spain
August 20, 1749

[Excerpt from the letter to Father Francesch Serra (probably a distant cousin)]

Friend of my heart: At this moment, words fail me, trying to express my feelings, as I bid you farewell, nor can I properly ask again the favor of your consoling my parents who, I not doubt, need it in their suffering. I wish I could share with them the great joy that fills my heart. Surely then they would encourage me to move forward and never turn back. May they

---

26 *Lands of Promise and Despair: Chronicles of Early California, 1535-1846*, ed. Rose Marie Beebe and Robert Senkewicz (Berkeley, CA: Heyday Books, 2001), 227.

27 Note: The extensive "Guide to Serrana" from the SBMAL can be found online. Another helpful resource is the Bibliography at the California Mission Studies Association website.

be advised that the actual work and practice of an Apostolic Preacher is the greatest calling which they could have wished for me . . .

Let my parents rejoice that they have a son who is a priest, though bad and sinful, who daily in the holy sacrifice of the Mass prays for them with all the fervor of his soul and on many days says Mass for them alone, that the Lord may help them; that they may not lack their daily bread; that He may give them patience in their trials, resignation to His holy will, peace and union with everyone, courage to fight the temptations of the evil one, and last of all, when it is God's will, a calm death in His holy grace. If I, by the grace of God, succeed in becoming a good religious, my prayers will become more potent, and they, in turn, will reap the benefit.[28]

Clearly Serra is responding to God's call. What did he have to gain by leaving his home? It is safe to assume that he gained a more profound understanding to his vows of poverty, chastity, and obedience to God, His Church, and Her people. He always moved forward, choosing never to turn back.

May 15, 1769

[Excerpt from diary entry, on the Sacred Expedition from Loreto to San Diego; encountering pre-contact natives for the first time]

I saw what I could not hardly believe when I would read about it or when I would be told about it, which was that the gentiles were totally naked, like Adam in paradise before the fall. That is how they went about and that is how they presented themselves to us. We interacted with them for quite some time and not once did they show any sign of embarrassment seeing that we were clothed and they were not. I placed my hands on the head of each gentile, one at a time, as a sign of affection. I filled both of their hands with overripe figs, which they immediately began to eat. We received a gift from them and with signs we showed them how much we appreciated it. The gift was a net full of mescal and four beautiful fish,

---

28 Orfalea, 67–68.

which were more than medium size. Unfortunately, the poor people had not thought to clean the fish beforehand or even to salt them, so the cook said the fish were not any good. Padre Campa also gave them his raisins, the Señor Gobernador gave them tobacco leaves, and all the soldiers received them warmly and gave them food to eat.[29]

Serra does not sound like a man bent on destruction of the other. A coming together of two cultures takes place and an exchange is made. One learns from the other. It reminds me of when I visited the Philippines for the first time. I was definitely out of my comfort zone, but willing to learn.

June 12, 1770
Carmel

[Excerpt from letter to Father Juan Andrés, Superior at College of San Fernando]

Our arrival was greeted by the joyful sound of the bells suspended on the branches of the oak tree. Everything being in readiness, and having put on alb and stole, and kneeling down with all the men before the altar having toned the hymn Veni, Creator Spiritus *[Come Holy Spirit, Creator Blest], at the conclusion of which, and after invoking the help of the Holy Spirit on everything we were about to perform, I blessed the salt and the water. Then we all made our way to a gigantic cross which was all in readiness and lying on the ground. With everyone lending a hand, we set it in the ground and then, with all the tenderness of our hearts, we venerated it. I sprinkled with holy water all the fields around. And thus, after raising aloft the standard of the King of Heaven, we unfurled the flag of our Catholic Monarch likewise. As we raised each one of them, we shouted at the top of our voices, "Long live the faith! Long live the King!"*[30]

---

29 "On the Road to San Diego: Junípero Serra's Baja California Diary," trans. Rose Marie Beebe and ed. Robert Senkewicz, *The Journal of San Diego History*, Fall 2013, 206.
30 *Lands of Promise and Despair: Chronicles of Early California, 1535–1846*, 140.

Clearly one can see the patronage system at work here. But note Serra's primary reliance on the Holy Spirit.

Serra to Viceroy Bucareli
August 24, 1774

From rancherias very far distant, and lost in the folds of the mountains, they arrive every day . . . they [natives] *tell us frankly how delighted they would be if they had Fathers in their country. They see the church and how attractive it looks; they see the cornfields which appear wonderful in their eyes; they see the throngs of children and all the rest of the people, how they are all clothed, and sing and eat in plenty, even though they have to work. All this, together with the working of our Lord in their souls, who doubts that this wins their hearts.*[31]

Some do doubt this today. Why, though? Cynicism, skepticism, anger, distrust? I turn again to the obvious question, what would Serra gain by lying?

Serra to Viceroy Bucareli
September 9, 1774

[Excerpt, referring to an earlier letter and providing an update]

I gave to your Excellency, also, the agreeable tidings that these new Christians [neophytes], *following the example set by some of the crews of the vessels whose services I managed to secure, are learning how to apply themselves to labor, how in hand and with the bar in making adobes, in harvesting the maize and the wheat and in carting these crops, as well as in other work in which they take part. I reported, also, that this year there have been harvested at this mission, in addition to twenty fanegas of barley, one-hundred and twenty-five of wheat, together with some horse-beans and a greater quantity of kidney-beans, and continuous crops from the vegetable garden — in the consumption of which all share. There is reason for expecting a fair return from the maize sown, and it is now*

---

31 Junípero Serra, 2:141.

well-grown and in good condition, and there will be obtained a goodly number of fish from the abundance of sardines which, for twenty consecutive days, have been spawning along the beach near this mission, and a reasonable harvest from the spiritual advancement we are experiencing each day — thanks be to God! At all the missions preparations are making for more extensive sowings in the coming year, and I trust in God that a happy outcome may attend the work. [32]

I included this for reflection for the sole reason to be mindful of, at least during this moment in time, diverse persons were working together for the common good.

Report on the Mission of San Carlos de Borromeo July 1, 1784

[Written eight weeks before his death; it is a year-to-year overview of the mission system under his leadership; these excerpts are for the year 1783]

We can consider this the happiest year of the mission because the number of baptisms was one hundred seventy-five and of marriages thirty-six.

The sowing of all grains amounted to eighty-four bushels, eight pecks. This included one bushel and a half of wheat, half a bushel of corn, and two pecks of beans, which were sown for the [Old] California Indians, who had moved here and were married in this mission . . .

Today the new Christians of this mission number six hundred fourteen living persons, even though some take leave from time to time . . .

The condition, then, of the Mission in things spiritual is that up to this day in this Mission:

Baptisms	*1,006*
Confirmations[33]	*936*

---

32 James R. Moriarty, "Father Serra and the Soldiers," *The Journal of San Diego History,* vol. 13, no. 3. July 1967, accessed February 13, 2013, http://www.sandiegohistory.org/journal/67july/serra.htm, 6.

33 Note: Due to geographic hindrances, Serra was granted a dispensation to perform the Sacrament that is customarily done by a Bishop. California would not have its first bishop until 1842.

And since those of the other missions belong in some way to this it is noted in passing that their number is 5,307

Marriages in this mission	*259*
Burials	*356*

The number of Christian families living at the mission and eating jointly, as well as widowers, single men, and children of both sexes, is evident from the enclosed census lists and is omitted here.

They pray twice daily with the priest in the church. More than one hundred twenty of them confess in Spanish and many who have died used to do as well. The others confess as best they can. They work at all kinds of mission labor, such as farm hands, herdsmen, cowboys, shepherds, milkers, diggers, gardeners, carpenters, farmers, irrigators, reapers, blacksmiths, sacristans, and they do everything else that comes along for their corporal and spiritual welfare.[34]

Serra's last will and testament is evidence of a life well lived, one devoted to building up the kingdom of God and the good of others. His worthiness to be counted among the communion of Saints seems inevitable.

Tapestry, Our Lady of Angels Cathedral, Los Angeles, California. Serra is second from left.

Photo by TERRY RUSCIN

---

34 *Documents of American Catholic History*, ed. John Tracy Ellis. (Milwaukee: The Bruce Publishing Company, 1956), 44–49.

CHAPTER 7

Legacy

On August 28, 1784, Junípero Serra no longer suffered for love, dying at Mission San Carlos Borromeo. Father Palóu describes the reaction to Serra's death.

> The doors [of the church] were now thrown open, and the Indians tendered bouquets of wild flowers, which were deposited by the donors at the feet of the revered body, which remained at the same spot until night, constantly visited by the awestruck multitude. The devout touched his hands with rosaries, calling him 'Holy Father,' 'blessed,' and other names indicative of his virtue. About dusk the Christian Indians, soldiers and sailors carried the body in procession to the church and placed it on a table, around which burned six wax candles. In compliance with the general demand, the door was left open all night, and devout groups took turns in watching and reciting rosary; two soldiers were put on guard, and though strict orders were given that no one should touch Father Junipero's body or habit, nevertheless, the next day it was found that several pieces of his habit had been removed, and also portions of his hair. On Sunday, August 29th, a solemn Requiem mass was sung, at which were present the Captain of the packet-boat, the marine officers, the Chaplain, Diaz, and military. Every half-hour cannons were fired and the funeral bells tolled mournfully.[35]

---

35 Palóu, 135-136.

What happened to the missions after Serra's death? During my lengthy quest I found that those who throw stones at the Church during the Mission era have the burden of proof. They seem emotionally driven. If they only took the time to get to know Junípero the man, they would find he lived up to his name that loosely translates to "fool of Christ."

The Franciscans toiled in New California from 1769 until 1831. They were called to this part of the world to share the good news of Jesus Christ. They worked in conjunction with the Spanish crown. This was sometimes an uneasy relationship due to the question of what was more important — the material or spiritual. Both are important in living out the gospel, yet some feel they have to make a choice. It was this tension that impacted the native neophyte and non-Christian.

James D. Hart, professor at University of California, Berkeley for fifty-four years wrote in *A Companion to California,*

> Conversion of members of the tribes who came to be called Mission Indians was slow; by 1774 the first five missions had baptized fewer than 500 infants and enrolled under 500 members, averaging fewer than 40 persons annually for each missionary. But difficulties also came from poor supply lines, insufficient equipment and food, strained and bureaucratic relations with Mexico, and problems in converting and controlling the generally docile but sometimes hostile Indians.[36]

The natives who freely entered the mission came into contact with a whole new way of life. In many ways it would be like people of the twenty-first century encountering beings from another planet. The padres and soldiers were building a "little Spain" in the farthest outpost of the empire. To ensure success, Spanish colonists were needed in order to keep others, especially Russia and England, at bay. Farming and husbandry transformed the natives, who once spent most of their day

---

36 James D. Hart, *A Companion to California* (Oxford University Press: New York, 1978), 276.

hunting, fishing, and gathering. Permanent structures of adobe were built. Following education on the basic beliefs of Catholic Christianity, they put on white robes — signifying purity — and were baptized. The convert was expected to now have a new mind and heart that was to always be open to the transforming power of Christ. French Navy officer and explorer La Pérouse wrote in his diary while visiting Monterey and San Carlos Borromeo Mission for ten days in 1786, "It must be observed that the moment an Indian is baptized, the effect is the same as if he pronounced a vow for life."[37] They were also granted Spanish citizenship and the rights and responsibilities that came with it. One can only imagine that some were sincere in their conversion while others were not. Some neophytes who returned to their old homes wanted to remain. Soldiers and neophytes would be sent to retrieve them after they extended the stay that was written out for them when the request was made. The padres' main goal was to help the neophytes remain true to the faith and not revert to their previous lives. Salvation of souls was paramount. Also, in order to keep law and order, corporal punishment was used. Steven Hackel said in an interview after Serra's canonization was announced, "Spanking or some sort of physical aggressiveness was their [Spaniards] way of correcting wayward people. And, of course, in today's world we would consider that to be unacceptable"[38] Corporal punishment was common throughout Spain and her territories and even in the United States until the mid-twentieth century.

The missions had good, lean, and in-between years. One certainty is they provided the neophyte new homes. The padre viewed the neophyte as their children and cared for their spiritual and material needs. The natives were the reason for the missions. They were not slaves. Catholic Spain had tried to eradicate slavery since the New Laws of 1542. The

---

37 Randall Milliken, *A Time of Little Choice: The Disintegration of Tribal Culture in the San Francisco Bay 1769-1810* (Menlo Park, CA: Ballena Press, 1995), 95.

38 "Historian Weighs In On Pope's Surprise Decision To Canonize A Controversial Californian Friar," CBS Los Angeles, January 15, 2015, accessed February 22, 2015, http://losangeles.cbslocal.com/2015/01/15/exclusive-pope-francis-to-canonize-friar-junipero-serra-during-us-visit/.

Spanish did not have the manpower for military force or religious co-ercion. Historian and longtime curator of Southern California history at the Los Angeles County Museum of Natural History William Marvin Mason presents some telling **demographics**. Here is a general picture.

It was estimated in 1795 that within the range of the missions (500-600 miles long and 50-60 miles wide) lived 20,000 natives.[39] By 1790, eleven of the twenty-one missions had been founded. Also of note, all four presidi-os, or forts, were in place (San Diego and Monterey, 1769; San Francisco, 1776; Santa Barbara, 1782). In 1782, San Diego had fifty-two soldiers, and 1783 Monterey had a garrison of fifty-six, San Francisco thirty-three, and Santa Barbara sixty-one.[40] The 1790 census reported 211 men having the occupation of soldier.[41] Each mission, not near a presidio, usually had five soldiers.[42] By 1808, thirty-two years after the Anza Expedition — consist-ing of 240 settlers — arrived in San Francisco after a 1,800 mile trek from present-day Mexico, there were 1,950 colonial Californians.[43] Supply ships from San Blas in Old California were a rarity.

During the Mexican era (1821-1848) there were a string of twenty-one missions, from San Diego in the south to Sonoma in the north. When the last mission closed its doors in 1836, due to the **Secularization** Law passed in 1834 by the Mexican Congress, 142 Franciscan priests would have lived in New California at some point. Native revolts were more common after 1824 — the time of transition from Spanish rule to Mexican.[44] The missions needed financial support from the monarchy. The goal was that the missions would be self-sufficient in ten years. For many reasons, that never bore true. The years following 1808 were a

---

39 William Marvin Mason, *The Census of 1790: A Demographic History of Colonial California* (Menlo Park, CA: Ballena Press, 1998), 2.
40 Ibid, 77–98.
41 Ibid, 73.
42 Ibid, 74.
43 Ibid, 44.
44 Andrew Rolle and Arthur Verge, *California: A History*, seventh edition (Wheeling, IL: Harlan Davidson, Inc., 2008), 72.

time ripe with fear of the unknown for the Spanish citizen living in New California as New Spain struggled to strengthen their settlements.

Mexico took possession of New California in 1821 and life became more challenging. The missions were eventually secularized and turned into parish churches for the pueblos, or towns. Hart continues,

> By 1833 some 31,000 Indians still lived in such settings under a temporal and spiritual despotism, not always benevolent, controlled by only 60 padres and 300 soldiers. By that date almost 88,000 Indians had been baptized and over 24,000 had been married by Catholic ritual.[45]

According to records at The Early California Population Project,[46] Serra's legacy was 101,000 baptisms, 28,000 marriages and 71,000 burials at all 21 missions and from the Los Angeles Plaza Church and the Santa Barbara Presidio. His dedication clearly shows that he took very seriously the words he wrote home from Cadiz, "forward and never turn back." However, when the first Bishop of Alta California, Francisco Garcia Diego y Moreno, arrived at Santa Barbara on January 11,

San Mateo Asistencia (outpost or rancho), founded ca. 1793.

Image Source: Stanger, 247-258.

1842, there were only seventeen Franciscan Fathers, mostly aged and infirm, to minister to the people at the twenty-one secularized Indian missions and six Spanish towns.

---

45 James D. Hart, 276.

46 "Early California Population Project," The Huntington Library, 2006, accessed February 11, 2015, http://www.huntington.org/information/ECPPabout.htm.

Disease, particularly measles, smallpox and syphilis, was the greatest contributor to native Christian deaths. In the early twentieth century, cultural anthropologist A.L. Kroeber and **physiologist** S.F. Cook did not agree on the native population before colonization. Most estimates today put the native population in California at 100,000 for the years 1769 to 1822.[47] Kroeber and Cook did agree that the missions saw numbers plummet, the greatest coming in the measles epidemic of 1806, and that another major drop would occur in 1850 after California became the thirty-first state in the United States. Andrew Galvan, Ohlone Indian and curator at Mission San Francisco de Asís, stated in a 2011 article on the Serra sainthood cause: "Serra's papers show he asked what was done in Spain when children were not thriving. Give them more milk, the answer came. Still, children died. Later, science would show that the native coastal people were lactose-intolerant, something Serra could hardly have known three centuries ago."[48] The mission system was poorly financed in an empire that became too big to govern. Colonists who took on a new identity called mestizo (through **amalgamation** – native and Spaniards intermarrying) saw this and revolution ensued in New Spain. In short, Spain was far away, its influence was spread thin, and people began to see themselves less and less as Spaniard.

Post-Mission period, the treatment of the native in the United States was abysmal, and in California it was frightening. During the Gold Rush era and as late as 1871, actions supported by the California government fit our modern definition of **genocide** (adopted by the United Nations in 1948).[49] In 1900, seventy-eight years after the American period of trading with the missions began, the population fell from 100,000 to 15,377.

---

47 Rolle and Verge, 14.

48 Michelle Jurich, "Mission curator hopeful as Serra sainthood cause just one miracle away." *Catholic San*
    Francisco, April 1, 2011, 10.

49 Note: For a detailed look at this period of California history, see Dr. Gayle Olson-Raymer, Humboldt State University, Department of History, "Americanization and the California Indians - A Case Study of Northern California," accessed March 9, 2015, http://users.humboldt.edu/ogayle/hist383/CaliforniaIndians.html.

In 1853 Bishop Sadoc Alemany asked the United States government to return the mission lands taken by the Mexican government to the Church. It was not until 1865, just months before his assassination, that Abraham Lincoln did so.

The triumph and tragedy of the missions can be summarized in one man's story — Pablo Tac. Pablo was a Luiseño. He was born at Mission San Luis Rey de Francia, one of six children, and baptized shortly after his birth on January 15, 1822. He and another boy, Agapito Amamix, were recognized by Father Peyri for their promise as students. When the priest decided to leave California in 1832, he took them to Mexico. They would then go to Rome and be registered at the Urban College (devoted to teaching future missionary priests) on September 23, 1834. There they began a four-year course in Latin grammar. Agapito

Sketch by Pablo Tac

fell ill and died on September 26, 1837. Pablo would finish his grammar course and studied rhetoric, humanities, and philosophy from 1838 until 1841. However, in 1840 he became ill with smallpox. After a short respite, he became sick again, dying on December 13, 1841, before he could achieve his dream of being a missionary priest.

Pablo left us with two sources that shed light on his native people during the mission period. A custom at the college was for students to recite poems in their native language. In order to do this effectively, Pablo prepared a partial vocabulary book in his native language, a way of writing Luiseño that drew on Latin and Spanish. The other source is a short document titled "Conversion of the San Luiseños of Alta California," probably written soon after he arrived at Urban College. This writing is a gem, giving us insight into mission life like no other can — from the native perspective. He writes of life before the Spanish; the arrival of the Spaniards; the building of the Mission, gardens and environs; administration of the Mission; and daily life for those who lived at the Mission, including dancing, and games. Pablo's concluding thoughts on the section about the arrival of the Spaniards were; "O merciful God, why didst Thou leave us for many centuries, years, months, and days in utter darkness after Thou camest to the world? Blessed be Thou from this day through future centuries."[50] These words tug at the human heart. So bittersweet.

---

50 Pablo Tac, *Indian Life and Customs at Mission San Luis Rey: A Record of California Mission Life*, **Ethnology** *of the Alta California Indians II: Postcontact*, ed. Lowell John Bean and Sylvia Brakke Vane (New York: Garland Publishing, Inc., 1991), 149.

CHAPTER 8

How did we get here?

We all need heroes. It is in our nature. Thomas Jefferson, Franklin Delano Roosevelt, Ty Cobb, and Reverend Martin Luther King, Jr. are some that I admire for their great achievements. However, I am well aware of their humanity. Jefferson owned slaves, FDR ordered the forced internment of Japanese Americans, Cobb, the baseball great, was often violent and a racist, and MLK had infidelity issues. Their lives seem paradoxical, maybe even hypocritical. For Roman Catholics, our heroes are called saints (from the Latin *sancti*, "holy ones"). We believe they intercede on our behalf and bring our prayers to God. We have that human connection with them, because they too were human and all that entails. The *Catechism of the Catholic Church* offers this beautiful description of a saint from the Second Vatican Council: "By doing the will of the Father in everything, with our whole heart for the glory of God and service to our neighbor" (2013). All Christians are called to this holiness in our common baptism with all of our faults. We must, first, choose to be holy.

The Church feels confident that some who have gone before us lived holy lives to a heroic degree — saints. The process of canonization is very formal. It is conducted by the Congregation for the Causes of Saints. The predecessor of the congregation was the Sacred Congregation for Rites, founded by Pope Sixtus V on January 22, 1588. Before that, martyrs were recognized by the faithful as saints. The process has gradually developed for roughly 2000 years to what it is today.

I will simplify the process that is actually governed in canon law by using as an analogy, my favorite baseball team the San Francisco Giants organization. What do they have in common? One has to work one's way through the farm leagues before making it to the bigs.

A – Augusta (GA) GreenJackets Lake Olmstead Stadium (cap. 4,882)	SERVANT OF GOD The local church where the person lived recognizes that the person was a living saint during their lifetime. They want to share his or her story with the universal Church. The person must have been deceased for at least five years. This is done in consultation with the local bishop. He has the final say to its legitimacy. If approved the cause is sent to the Congregation at the Vatican.
AA – Richmond (VA) Flying Squirrels The Diamond (cap. 9, 560)	VENERABLE When the Congregation, after confirming the proposal from the local bishop, brings it to the pope. After his confirmation, the person in question is known as "heroic in virtue."
AAA – Sacramento (CA) River Cats Raley Field (cap. 14,014)	BLESSED When the pope states that it is "worthy of belief" that the person is in heaven. One miracle has been confirmed. In modern times, it is almost always medical, something that science cannot explain. This stage is known as beatification. In regard to Serra, in 1960 a Novena Prayer began to Serra on behalf of Sister Dyrda. She was cured of lupus.
MLB – San Francisco Giants AT&T Park (cap. 41,915)	SAINT In the strictest sense, this occurs when a second prayer to the person has been answered through a miracle. The pope does have the authority to dispense of this requirement because this is a rule made by man, not God, and people pray to the blessed as if they are a saint already anyway. This stage is known as canonization.

Raymond Starr, San Diego State University History professor emeritus, asserted in his 1989 book review of *The Missions of California: A Legacy of Genocide*, that, "Too often it is forgotten that Serra aimed not just to convert the Indians to Catholicism but to eradicate Indian culture as well."[51] How does one make sense out of the saint-or-sinner proposition?

---

51 Raymond Starr, "Book Review: The Missions of California," *The Journal of San Diego History*, vol. 35, no. 3. Summer 1989, accessed July 3, 2014, http://www.sandiegohistory.org/journal/89summer/br-missions.htm.

One person who helped clarify for me the saint-or-sinner rhetoric was Robert M. Senkewicz, professor of History at Santa Clara University. In his paper, "The Representation of Junípero Serra in California History," he shows the metamorphosis of perspectives and depictions of Serra through the years.

He begins with Father Francisco Palóu's biography, started just weeks after Serra's death. He writes, "Palóu's biography of Serra thus combined three purposes. As a personal document, it was an emotional and heartfelt tribute to a dear friend. As a religious document, it was an attempt to convince more Spanish Franciscans to become missionaries. As a political document, it was an attempt to convince the government to change its colonial policies. The biography succeeded in all three purposes."[52] He continues, "What was left was the personal picture he had painted of Junípero Serra—a dedicated, selfless missionary who did not allow personal hardship or pain to interfere with his desire to bring salvation and civilization to the Indians whom he loved."[53] According to Senkewicz, Franklin Tuthill's *History of California*, published in 1866, relied on Palóus work. Tuthill remarked, "Father Junípero Serra learned to love [the Indians] as if they were his own flesh."

Serra also had his detractors. John S. Hittell in *A History of San Francisco* (1878) wrote, "Junípero Serra was a typical Franciscan, a man to whom his religion was everything . . . . Art or poetry never served to sharpen his wits, lighten his spirits, or solace his weary moments. . . . He knew nothing of the science and philosophy which threw all enlightened nations into fermentation a hundred years ago."[54] Hubert Howe Bancroft (1832-1918 — the library at the University of California at Berkeley is named in his honor) was another. In his seven volume work

---

52 Robert M. Senkewicz. "The Representation of Junípero Serra in California History," in Rose Marie Beebe and Robert M Senkewicz, eds. *To Toil in That Vineyard of the Lord: Contemporary Scholarship on Junípero Serra* (Berkeley: Academy of American Franciscan History, 2010), 20.

53 Ibid, 21.

54 Ibid, 22.

on California history, he paints a picture of Serra as having an "arbitrary and unconciliating spirit" and a **bigot**.[55]

The major impact on how people perceived and understood Serra was through popular culture, known as the Spanish Revival movement. Two people in the movement are of particular importance. Senkewicz states the 1883 essay "Father Junípero Serra and His Work," by Helen Hunt Jackson, "helped set the stage for the heroic and sentimental view of Serra that became prevalent." Hunt wrote that Serra was, "the foremost, grandest figure in the mission's history. If his successors in their administration had been equal to him in spirituality, enthusiasm, and intellect, the mission establishments would never have been so utterly overthrown and ruined."[56] At the turn of the twentieth century, Angeleno Charles Fletcher Lummis, journalist and Native American

US Postal Service, 1969.

rights and historic preservation activist, was Serra and the missions greatest advocate. He was so adamant that Spain's achievements be included in the collective American narrative that it became much of his lifelong work. His efforts would even be recognized with an award from King Alfonso XIII of Spain. A May 11, 1902, *Los Angeles Herald* article succinctly describes Lummis' love for the padres and the missions. During the lecture he gave to the mission preservation group that he founded, the Landmarks Club, he said of the friars and the work they did; ". . . we must respect and honor them, whatever be our creeds." It was pretty clear to Lummis, the son of a Methodist minister from New England, that the Spanish missions were something very special.

In 1931 the Empire State building was opened, Herbert Hoover was President, the Star Spangled Banner was adopted as the national anthem and Mayor of San Francisco James Rolph, Jr. was given the go

---

55 Ibid, 24.
56 Ibid, 26-27.

ahead monies from the federal government to begin construction of the San Francisco-Oakland Bay Bridge. It was also the year that Serra was memorialized with a statue in the rotunda of the United States Capitol (each state can select two significant people from their state to honor). The movement began in 1910, its major booster the Native Sons of the Golden West, an organization with a history of historical preservation. It was a big deal. Bishop Shahan, rector of the Catholic University of America, gave the invocation. The United States Marine Corps Band played patriotic songs and speeches were given by politicians. Father Muller, representing the Franciscan Friars of California, summed up the popular sentiment for Serra in the early part of the twentieth century: "The unveiling of the statue of Junípero Serra is the realization of the words spoken by the Hon. Hiram W. Johnson when on the 24th of November, 1913, the bicentennial of the birth of Junípero Serra, as Governor of the State of California he proclaimed a legal holiday saying: 'To the memory of Junípero Serra California owes an everlasting tribute. He brought civilization to our land, and in deed and character he deserves a foremost place in the history of our State.'"[57]

Events like the Trail of Tears in 1838 and Wounded Knee on December 29, 1890, were not forgotten. *The Americas*, a quarterly review of Latin American History published by the Academy of American Franciscan History, presented an article in 1963 by Native American historian Jack D. Forbes titled "The Historian and the Indian: Racial **Bias** in American History." The understanding portrayed by Father Francis J. Weber in the 1966 preface to *A Select Guide to California Catholic History* began to be challenged. Weber wrote, "Telling the story of California's missions is no new endeavor and the pageantry of that era is now an accepted and pivotal part of Western Americana. Through the dedicated efforts of such scholars as Zephyrin Engelhardt, Herbert E. Bolton, and Maynard J. Geiger, quality has been combined with quantity to

---

57 *The Statues of Junípero Serra and Thomas Starr King* (Washington, D.C.: United States Government Printing Office, 1932), 56.

provide narratives at once accurate and absorbing."[58]

The American Indian Movement was organized in 1968. Seventy-nine members even occupied the closed Federal Penitentiary at Alcatraz in San Francisco Bay from November 20, 1969, to June 11, 1971. They protested years of harsh treatment, distrust, and being shut out of the mainstream (Native Americans were not allowed United States citizenship until 1924). In other words, frustration in the Native American community boiled over, and their voice was beginning to be heard – some even expressing dissatisfaction about Serra and the California missions.

Senkewicz argues that, "The interpretations [of Serra] were often guided by the cultural concerns of the eras in which they were constructed." He continues, "Historical figures are inevitably interpret-

Serra Statue, National Statuary Hall, US Capitol, Washington, D.C.

Photo by KEVIN CAREY

ed through the prism of the present, whenever that present might be, and even canonized saints are not exempt from this rule."[59] This sense of presentism, though, shields one from the truth. That aside, wounds do exist. The Church teaches we are all children of God, brothers and sisters under the skin. What has she done to help heal the wounds?

According to the United States Conference of Catholic Bishops, Secretariat of Cultural Diversity report, "Native Americans at the Millennium," 116,000 (or 20%) of the 580,000 Native Americans are Roman Catholic Christian (3.5% of all Roman Catholics in the United

---

58 Francis J. Weber, *A Select Guide to California Catholic History* (Los Angeles: Westernlore Press, 1966), xiiii.

59 Senkewicz, 51-52.

States).[60] They are the legacy of Serra and other great missionaries such as Jean de Brébeuf, Pierre-Jean DeSmet, Francisco Garcés, Eusebio Kino, and Jacques Marquette.

Pope John Paul II came to the United States in 1987, visiting Phoenix, Arizona, on September 14. After watching and listening to traditional native song and dance, he shared the following with the 16,000 Catholic American Indians representing more than 200 tribes at Arizona Memorial Coliseum.

> The early encounter between your traditional cultures and the European way of life was an event of such significance and change that it profoundly influences your collective life even today. That encounter was a harsh and painful reality for your peoples. The cultural oppression, the injustices, the disruption of your life and of your traditional societies must be acknowledged. At the same time, in order to be objective, history must record the deeply positive aspects of your peoples' encounter with the culture that came from Europe. Among these positive aspects, I wish to recall the work of the many missionaries who strenuously defended the rights of the original inhabitants of this land. They established missions throughout this Southwestern part of the United States. They worked to improve living conditions and set up educational systems, learning your languages in order to do so. Above all, they proclaimed the good news of salvation in our Lord Jesus Christ, an essential part of which is that all men and women are equally children of God and must be respected and loved as such. This Gospel of Jesus Christ is today, and

60 "2013 Tekakwitha Conference Convention; Plus: Native American Stats," Indian Country Today Media Network, April 4, 2013, accessed January 29, 2015, http://indiancountrytodaymedianetwork.com/2013/04/14/2013-tekakwitha-conference-convention-plus-native-catholic-stats-148799.

will remain forever, the greatest pride and possession of your people."[61]

Father Michael Galvan, an Ohlone Indian and priest of the Diocese of Oakland (California), said of the visit, "It was a glorious event . . . important to the native people.[62]

The Pope would visit Carmel Mission Basilica, resting place of Junípero Serra, on September 17. The September 19, 1987, *San Francisco Chronicle* reported 2,500 people greeted Pope John Paul II. Thirty Indians and six pro-abortion demonstrators protested outside. He concluded the homily saying;

In him who is the source of my strength, I have strength for everything (Philippians 4:13). These words of the great missionary, Saint Paul, remind us that our strength is not our own. Even in the martyrs and saints, as the liturgy reminds us, it is "[God's] power shining through our human weakness" (Preface of Martyrs). It is the strength that inspired Father Serra's motto: "Always forward, never back." It is the strength that one senses in this place of prayer so filled with his presence. It is the strength that can make each one of us, dear brothers and sisters, missionaries of Jesus Christ, witnesses of His message, doers of His word.[63]

Though reconciliation was the spirit of the day during the pope's visit, the old canards of Serra being a religious zealot and genocidal

61 John Paul II, Papal Address, Meeting with the Native Peoples of the Americas, September 14, 1987, accessed February 14, 2015, http://w2.vatican.va/content/john-paul-ii/en/speeches/1987/september/documents/hf_jp-ii_spe_19870914_amerindi-phoenix.html.

62 Teresa Schuelke, "On behalf of her people," *The Message*, December 25, 1987, accessed February 11, 2015, http://mes.stparchive.com/Archive/MES/MES12251987P06.php.

63 "Address on Father Junípero Serra and Evangelization," *¡Siempre Adelante! The Newsletter for the Cause of Blessed Junípero*, Spring/Summer 2007, accessed February 14, 2015, https://sbfranciscans.org/sites/default/files/SiempreAdelante%20SpringSummer07_0.pdf.

maniac heard then returned in 2015 immediately after Pope Francis announced that Serra, whom he called the "evangelizer of the West," would be canonized. Only days after Pope Francis' announcement, California State Senator Ricardo Lara (D-Bell Gardens) called to replace the Serra statue in the National Statuary Hall. Bishop Robert McElroy of the Diocese of San Diego would remind all in an April 15, 2015 *San Diego Union-Tribune* article that Serra is a "foundational figure" in California history. He noted that the statue should remain as a testament not only to the past, but also the present. In 2013, 38.4% of Californians are Hispanic or Latino, according to the United States Census Bureau. Also, during Easter Sunday Mass more than 100 Native Americans peacefully protested the canonization of Serra at Carmel Mission Basilica.

The following objectively sheds light on life at a mission. In 2004, Robert L. Hoover, an **archaeologist** and a non-Catholic who spent twenty-eight years researching the missions of California, shared some reflections with *¡Siempre Adelante! The Newsletter for the Cause of Blessed Junípero Serra* on what he called ". . . Serra's remarkable efforts with the California Indians." He said,

> Joining a mission community freely and for whatever reason, the neophytes were protected from the labor demands of the military and civilian settlers. In exchange, they were expected to stay and contribute to the support of their own community. Mission production was communal property, and most of it was redistributed back into the mission community. When work was not required, neophytes were allowed to travel back to their home villages or hunt and gather in traditional ways. Labor requirements were reasonable, spread over a large number of people, and conducted according to a flexible schedule. Mission neophytes were not starved. Historical records and archaeological evidence of thousands of butchered and cooked animal bones indicate that

three balanced meals were provided each day, there was plenty of protein, and native foods continued to be eaten as snacks.[64]

William A. Haviland, Professor of **Anthropology** at the University of Vermont, states, "All cultures change over time . . . Changes occur in response to events such as environmental crises, the intrusion of outsiders, or the modification of behavior and values within the culture."[65] Regarding change and the native in California, anthropologist Randall Milliken shares, "The vast majority of them [natives] made that decision [to leave their homelands], in the absence of direct physical threat from the European intruders. Yet there can be no doubt that they made that decision during a time when changes in their world seemed to leave them little choice to do otherwise."[66] One thing seems certain, Native American life in New California changed after the Spanish came. It was almost totally annihilated shortly after the Gold Rush and American statehood.

---

64 Robert L. Hoover, *¡Siempre Adelante! The Newsletter for the Cause of Blessed Junípero Serra*, Santa Barbara, CA: Old Santa Barbara Mission, Spring/Summer 2004.

65 William A. Haviland, *Cultural Anthropology*, 9th edition (New York Harcourt Brace & Company, 1999), 52.

66 Randall Milliken, xiv.

CHAPTER 9

Conclusion

My dad was a history major and passed on to me his passion for the past. He taught me so much about the history of the Irish in America. When I was in high school, though, I remember asking my dad something like, "If the Irish did so much to help America, then why is there only one page in my history textbook devoted to their contributions?" He answered with words of sage advice that has proven useful throughout my life; "Go to the library and find out for yourself." This challenge to a quest has been a gift.

My quest has helped me to imagine the following. The Congregation for the Causes of Saints had a canon lawyer who had the title Devil's Advocate (the position existed from 1587 to 1983). His job was to find any reason for why the person should not be considered a saint. Imagine if the Devil's Advocate was on the flight with Pope Francis to Manila when he announced that Junípero Serra would be canonized. What would he have said to the Pope? Maybe the skeptic would say something to the effect, "Serra called the native a *pagan* and *children,* allowed for corporal punishment to be used to discipline errant ways, taught Spanish culture at the expense of native culture." He would cry out, "This would not be tolerated in this day and age! It even left the eighteenth century enlightened European visitor to the missions, like La Pérouse, dismayed. How can a Catholic today ask the likes of him to bring one's prayers to God?" Pope Francis, we can imagine, replies, "Oh you of little faith. Serra was a man of his time who embodied the Paschal Mystery. He put others before self. Yet he too went to confession. Was he a good Catholic? No. He was a great Catholic! He took to heart every word of Jesus; "You shall love the Lord your God with all your heart, with all your soul, and with all your mind. This is the greatest and the first commandment. The second is like it: You shall love your neighbor as yourself" (Mt 22:37–39).

My quest enabled me to see the forest for the trees when evaluating the history of Serra and the mission era. However, I had times of doubt, rejection, frustration and failure. But in the end it deepened my understanding of identity and meaning, making sense of the complex. Historian David McCollough reminds us of the importance of studying history. I paraphrase;

- It is not only important for the individual, but also for the community.
- We cannot truly know who we are or where we are going unless we know where we have been.
- It helps us value what our forebears have done for us.
- It will make us more thoughtful and understanding.
- We will behave better.
- It is joyful, connecting us to the shared experience of being alive.[67]

It is joyful, indeed.

In our digital age, the information available to us can be confusing. It is frustrating and discouraging to hear Serra's name and words like *enslaver, genocidal, forceful, exploiter, sadistic, brutal, intolerant,* used in the same sentence. What would Serra have us do? I think he would say, first and foremost, to pray. Pray that all hearts and minds are transformed to embrace faith, hope, and love in and through Christ. Next, be a twenty-first century missionary, or what Pope Francis calls

---

67 David McCollough, "History and Knowing Who We Are," *American Heritage,* vol. 58:3, Winter 2008, accessed February 14, 2015, http://www.americanheritage.com/content/history-and-knowing-who-we-are.

an informal preacher. He shares in *The Joy of the Gospel*, "[This] takes place in the middle of a conversation, something along the lines of what a missionary does when visiting a home. Being a disciple means being constantly ready to bring the love of Jesus to others, and this can happen unexpectedly and in any place: on the street, in a city square, during work, on a journey."[68] Last, recall the words of Sister Dyrda, the nun miraculously cured of lupus in 1960 after her friends prayed to Serra. Thomas G. Keene of the *San Francisco Chronicle* interviewed her September 16, 1987 at Carmel Mission Basilica, days before the papal visit. She said, "I only know that he [Serra] was a very saintly man and I pray to him every day." Then she knelt and prayed with several Natives staging a prayer vigil to protest Serra's alleged role in the demise of their culture.

Saint Michael the Archangel Mission. McGill, Nevada.

Window donated by Cathy and David Sandoval.

Photo by JENNIFER TALLERICO

There is a mission church named after Saint Michael the Archangel in McGill, Nevada (pop. 1,148). It was founded in 1910, to serve the Slav and Croat copper miners. If you had visited before September 2015 you would have surely noticed something peculiar. The stained glass window of Junípero Serra, installed in 1991, already gave him the title Saint. What a testament to the hope that Serra would one day be counted among the communion of saints.

---

68 Francis, Apostolic Exhortation, *The Joy of the Gospel* (Vatican City: Liberia Editrice Vaticana, 2013), 64.

Lord God,
Grant that we may always have open hearts and minds to see with
greater clarity that "the light shines in the darkness, and the darkness
has not overcome it" (Jn 1:5).
Saints Juan Diego, Kateri Tekakwitha, Issac Jogues, Katherine Drexel,
Junípero Serra,
Pray for Us!
Amen.

CHAPTER 10

Appendix

Glossary

amalgamation – when two or more cultures merge into a single, new culture. Alan G. Johnson, professor of Sociology, provides the example of Mexico as an amalgamation of Spanish and Native cultures (*The Blackwell Dictionary of Sociology* (Cambridge, MA: Basil Blackwell Inc. 1995), 64–65.

anthropology – the study of humans, past and present. To understand the full sweep and complexity of cultures across all of human history, anthropology draws and builds upon knowledge from the social and biological sciences as well as the humanities and physical sciences.

archaeology – the study of human activity in the past, primarily through the recovery and analysis of the material culture and environmental data that they have left behind, which includes artifacts, architecture, biofacts (also known as eco-facts), and cultural landscapes (the archaeological record).

bias – tendency to believe that some people, ideas, etc. are better than others that usually results in treating some unfairly.

bigot – one who is intolerant toward those holding different opinions.

Black Legend – a style of historical writing or propaganda that demonizes the Spanish Empire, its people and its culture (e.g. intolerant, cruel, violent religious fanatics).

bull – a particular type of letters patent or charter issued by a Pope of the Catholic Church. It is named after the lead seal (bulla) that was appended to the end in order to authenticate it.

demography – the statistical study of human populations.

encomienda – a grant by the Spanish Crown to a colonist in America conferring the right to demand tribute and forced labor from the Indian inhabitants of an area.

ethnology – the study of the characteristics of various peoples and the differences and relationships between them, ethnohistory is a discipline of ethnology. It is the study of cultures and indigenous customs by examining historical records as well as other sources of information on their lives and history. It is also the study of the history of various ethnic groups that may or may not exist today.

evangelize – to preach in word and deed the gospel, or good news, of Jesus the Christ.

Franciscan – people and groups (religious orders), formed in 1209, who adhere to the teachings and spiritual disciplines of Saint Francis of Assisi and adhere to the Roman Catholic Church.

genocide – the deliberate killing of a large group of people, especially those of a particular ethnic group or nation.

historian – an expert in or student of history, especially that of a particular period, geographical region, or social phenomenon.

Inquisition -- The Tribunal of the Holy Office of the Inquisition (Spanish: Tribunal del Santo Oficio de la Inquisición), commonly known as the Spanish Inquisition (Inquisición española), was established in 1478 by Catholic Monarchs Ferdinand II of Aragon and Isabella I of Castile. Marked by a period of prolonged and intensive questioning or investigation, it was intended to maintain Catholic orthodoxy in their kingdoms. The body was under the direct control of the Spanish monarchy. It was not definitively abolished until 1834, during the reign of Isabella II, after a period of declining influence in the previous century.

neophyte -- newly converted native.

physiology – the scientific study of normal function in living systems. A sub-discipline of biology, its focus is in how organisms, organ systems, organs, cells, and bio-molecules carry out the chemical or physical functions that exist in a living system.

priest – The whole Church is a priestly people. Through Baptism all the faithful share in the priesthood of Christ. This participation is called the "common priesthood of the faithful." Based on this common priesthood and ordered to its service, there exists another participation in the mission of Christ: the ministry conferred by the sacrament of Holy Orders, where the task is to serve in the name and in the person of Christ the Head in the midst of the community (*Catechism*, 1591).

secularization – division of the vast mission land holdings into land grants; churches were to become parishes, staffed by diocesan priests.

society – a group of people involved in persistent interpersonal relationships.

stereotypes – an often unfair and untrue belief.

viceroy – the regal official who ran New Spain in the name of and as representative of the monarch. The term derives from the Latin prefix vice, meaning "in the place of" and the French word *roi*, meaning king.

Maps

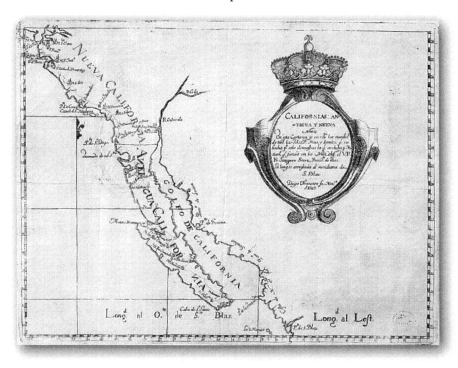

Map of California by Diego Troncoso

"Map of old and new California…made to demonstrate the travels of Father Fray Junípero Serra and the missions he founded and presided over in New California."

1787

Source: España. Ministerio de Cultura. Archivo General de Indias. MP-México, 706

New California
1784

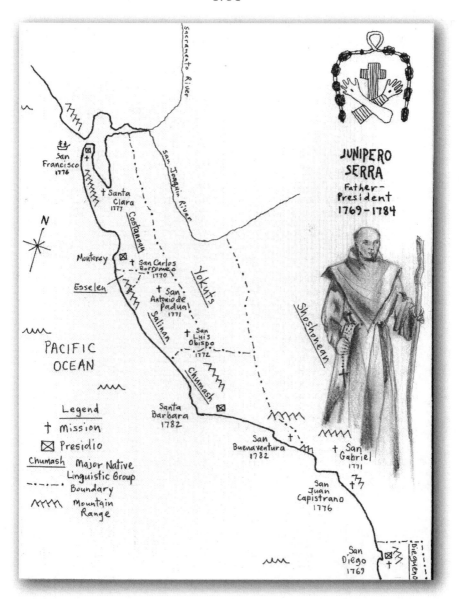

Sketch of Serra by Marco Hernandez

Timeline

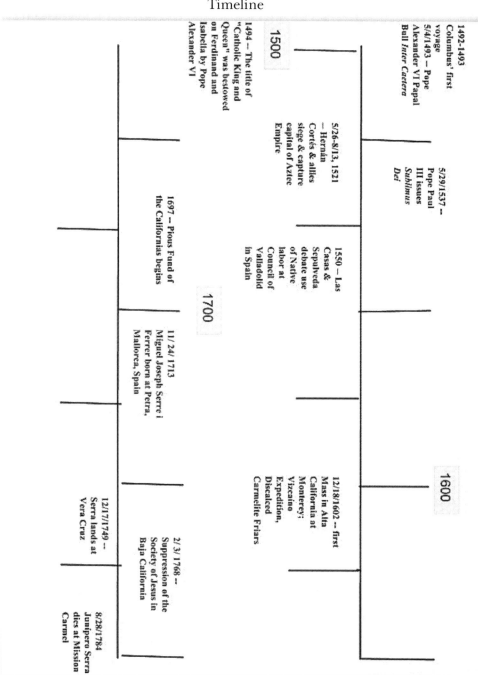

1492-1493
Columbus' first
voyage
5/4/1493 — Pope
Alexander VI Papal
Bull *Inter Caetera*

1494 — The title of
"Catholic King and
Queen" was bestowed
on Ferdinand and
Isabella by Pope
Alexander VI

1500

5/29/1537 —
Pope Paul
III issues
*Sublimus
Dei*

5/26-8/13, 1521
— Hernán
Cortés & allies
siege & capture
capital of Aztec
Empire

1550 — Las
Casas &
Sepúlveda
debate use
of Native
labor at
Council of
Valladolid
in Spain

12/18/1602 — first
Mass in Alta
California at
Monterey;
Vizcaíno
Expedition,
Discalced
Carmelite Friars

1600

1697 — Pious Fund of
the Californias begins

11/24/1713
Miguel Joseph Serre i
Ferrer born at Petra,
Mallorca, Spain

1700

12/17/1749 —
Serra lands at
Vera Cruz

2/3/1768 —
Suppression of the
Society of Jesus in
Baja California

8/28/1784
Junipero Serra
dies at Mission
Carmel

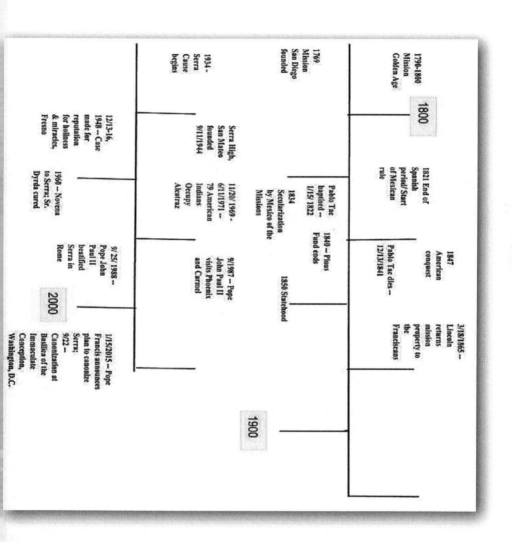

1790-1800
Mission
Golden Age

1769
Mission
San Diego
founded

1934 -
Serra
Cause
begins

1800

Serra High,
San Mateo
founded
9/11/1944

12/13-16,
1948 – Case
made for
reputation
for holiness
& miracles,
Fresno

1960 – Novena
to Serra; Sr.
Dyrda cured

1821 End of
Spanish
period/ Start
of Mexican
rule

1834
Secularization
by Mexico of the
Missions

Pablo Tac
baptised –
1/15/1822

11/20/1969 -
6/11/1971 –
79 American
Indians
Occupy
Alcatraz

9/25/1988 –
Pope John
Paul II
beatified
Serra in
Rome

2000

1840 – Plous
Fund ends

1847
American
conquest

Pablo Tac dies –
12/13/1841

1850 Statehood

9/1987 – Pope
John Paul II
visits Phoenix
and Carmel

3/18/1865 –
Lincoln
returns
mission
property to
the
Franciscans

1/15/2015 – Pope
Francis announces
plan to canonize
Serra;
9/23 –
Canonization at
Basilica of the
Immaculate
Conception,
Washington, D.C.

1900

CHAPTER 11

Bibliography

"Address on Father Junípero Serra and Evangelization," *¡Siempre Adelante! The Newsletter for the Cause of Blessed Junípero*, Spring/Summer 2007. Accessed February 14, 2015. https://sbfranciscans.org/sites/default/files/SiempreAdelante%20SpringSummer07_0.pdf.

Augustine, *Confessions*. San Bernardino, CA: Benton Press, 2013.

Basaraba, Sharon, "Longevity Throughout History: How has human life expectancy changed over time?" About.com. December 16, 2014. Accessed February 4, 2015. http://longevity.about.com/od/longevitystatsandnumbers/a/Longevity-Throughout-History.htm

"Blessed Junipero Serra," Franciscan Friars of the Province of Santa Barbara. Accessed February 11, 2015. https://sbfranciscans.org/about/blessed-junipero-serra.

Bloch, Marc. *The Historian's Craft*. Manchester, England: Manchester University Press, 2004.

California State Board of Education, History--Social Science Standards for California Public Schools. "Historical Analysis and Interpretations." Sacramento, CA: California Department of Education, 2000.

Catechism of the Catholic Church. 2nd ed. Vatican City: Libreria Editrice Vaticana, 2000.

Documents of American Catholic History. Edited by John Tracy Ellis. Milwaukee: The Bruce Publishing Company, 1956.

"Early California Population Project." The Huntington Library. 2006. Accessed February 11, 2015. http://www.huntington.org/information/ECPPabout.htm.

Francis. Apostolic Exhortation. *The Joy of the Gospel.* Vatican City: Liberia Editrice Vaticana, 2013.

Galgano, Robert. Review of Steven W. Hackel. *Children of Coyote, Missionaries of Saint Francis: Indian-Spanish Relations in Colonial California, 1769-1850.* H-Net Reviews. July 2006. Accessed February 14, 2015. http://www.hnet.org/reviews/showrev.php?id=11965.

Gallagher, Michael P. *Faith Maps: Ten Religious Explorers from Newman to Joseph Ratzinger.* New York: Paulist Press, 2010.

Geiger, Maynard. *Father Junípero Serra Paintings*, Mission San Luis Rey: Franciscan Friars, 1997.

Greenstein, Albert. "Fr. Junípero Serra." *The Historical Society of Southern California,* 1999. Accessed February 6, 2015. http://www.socalhistory.org/biographies/fr-junipero-serra.html.

Hackel, Steven W. *Junípero Serra: California's Founding Father.* New York: Hill and Wang, 2013.

Jedin, Hubert, ed. *Handbook of Church History*, Vol. 1, "General Introduction to Church History," Montreal: Palm Publishers, 1965.

Hart, James D. *A Companion to California*. New York: Oxford University Press, 1978.

Haviland, William A. *Cultural Anthropology*, 9th edition. New York: Harcourt Brace & Company, 1999.

"Historian Weighs In On Pope's Surprise Decision To Canonize A Controversial Californian Friar." CBS Los Angeles. January 15, 2015. Accessed February 22, 2015. http://losangeles.cbslocal. com/2015/01/15/exclusive-pope-francis-to-canonize-friar-junipero-serra-during-us-visit/.

Hoover, Robert L. *¡Siempre Adelante! The Newsletter for the Cause of Blessed Junípero Serra*. Santa Barbara, CA: Old Santa Barbara Mission, Spring/Summer 2004.

John Paul II. Encyclical Letter. *Veritatis splendor*. August 6, 1993. Accessed February 11, 2014. http://w2.vatican.va/content/john-paul-ii/en/encyclicals/documents/hf_jp-ii_enc_06081993_veritatis-splendor.html.

John Paul II. Papal Address. Meeting with the Native Peoples of the Americas. September 14, 1987. Accessed February 14, 2015. http://w2.vatican.va/content/john-paul-ii/en/speeches/1987/september/documents/hf_jp-ii_spe_19870914_amerindi-phoenix.html.

Jurich, Michelle. "Mission curator hopeful as Serra sainthood cause just one miracle away." *Catholic San Francisco*. April 1, 2011.

Lands of Promise and Despair: Chronicles of Early California, 1535-1846. Edited by Rose Marie Beebe and Robert Senkewicz. Berkeley, CA: Heyday Books, 2001.

McCollough, David. "History and Knowing Who We Are." *American Heritage*, vol. 58: 3. Winter 2008. Accessed February 14, 2015. http://www.americanheritage.com/content/history-and-knowing-who-we-are.

Mason, William Marvin. *The Census of 1790: A Demographic History of Colonial California*. Menlo Park, CA: Ballena Press, 1998.

Milliken, Randall. *A Time of Little Choice: The Disintegration of Tribal Culture in the San Francisco Bay Area 1769-1810*. Menlo Park, CA: Ballena Press, 1995.

Moriarty, James R. "Father Serra and the Soldiers." *The Journal of San Diego History* vol. 13, no. 3. July 1967. Accessed February 13, 2013. http://www.sandiegohistory.org/journal/67july/serra.htm.

"On the Road to San Diego: Junípero Serra's Baja California Diary." Translated by Rose Marie Beebe and Edited by Robert Senkewicz. *The Journal of San Diego History*. Fall 2013.

Orfalea, Gregory. *Journey to the Sun: Junípero Serra's Dream and the Founding of California*. New York: Scribner, 2014.

Palóu, Francisco, *Life of Venerable Father Junipero Serra: The First Apostle of California*, Translated by J. Adam. San Francisco: P.E. Dougherty & Co., 1884.

Pelowski, Alton. "Why Columbus Sailed." *Columbia*. May 24, 2014. Accessed February 4, 2015. http://www.kofc.org/en/columbia/detail/2012_06_columbus_interview.html.

"The Pope and Plato." *L'Osservatore Romano*. August 20, 2011. Accessed February 23, 2015. http://www.osservatoreromano.va/en/news/the-pope-and-plato.

Postel, Mitchell P. "Historic Resource Study for Golden Gate National Recreation Area in San Mateo County." National Park Service U.S. Department of the Interior, 2010. Accessed June 17, 2014. http://www.nps.gov/goga/historyculture/upload/San-Mateo-HRS-Introduction.pdf.

Pourade, Richard F. *The Explorers*. "Expeditions by Land." San Diego: The Union- Tribune Publishing Company, 1960, http://www.sandiegohistory.org/books/pourade/explorers/explorerschapter9.htm.

Ramírez, David Piñera. Translated by Anita Alvarez de Williams. "The Beginning of Secular Colonization in Baja California." *The Journal of San Diego History* 23, no. 1 (Winter 1977). Accessed February 4, 2015. http://www.sandiegohistory.org/journal/77winter/secular.htm.

Rolle, Andrew and Verge, Arthur. *California: A History*, seventh edition. Wheeling, IL: Harlan Davidson, Inc., 2008.

Schuelke, Teresa. "On behalf of her people." *The Message*. December 25, 1987. Accessed February 11, 2015. http://mes.stparchive.com/Archive/MES/MES12251987P06.php

Senkewicz, Robert M. "The Representation of Junípero Serra in California History." in Rose Marie Beebe and Robert M Senkewicz, eds. *To Toil in That Vineyard of the Lord: Contemporary Scholarship on Junípero Serra*. Berkeley: Academy of American Franciscan History, 2010.

Serra, Junípero. *Writings of Junípero Serra*, Vol. I. Ed. Antonine Tibesar. Washington, D.C.: Academy of American Franciscan History, 1955.

Stanger, Frank Merriman, "The Hospice" or "Mission San Mateo," *California Historical Society Quarterly* 23, no. 3, September 1944.

Starr, Raymond. "Book Review: The Missions of California," *The Journal of San Diego History*, vol. 35, no. 3. Summer 1989. Accessed July 3, 2014. http://www.sandiegohistory.org/journal/89summer/br-missions.htm.

The Statues of Junipero Serra and Thomas Starr King, Washington, D.C.: United States Government Printing Office, 1932.

Tac, Pablo. *Indian Life and Customs at Mission San Luis Rey: A Record of California Mission Life, Ethnology of the Alta California Indians II: Postcontact.* Edited by Lowell John Bean and Sylvia Brakke Vane. New York: Garland Publishing, Inc., 1991.

"2013 Tekakwitha Conference Convention; Plus: Native American Stats," Indian Country Today Media Network. April 4, 2013. Accessed January 29, 2015. http://indiancountrytodaymedianetwork.com/2013/04/14/2013-tekakwitha-conference-convention-plus-native-catholic-stats-148799

The Vatican Secret Archives. Antwerp, Belgium: VdH Books, 2009.

Weber, Francis J. *A Select Guide to California Catholic History.* Los Angeles: Westernlore Press, 1966.

Whitman, Walt. *Leaves of Grass.* New York: Penguin Classics, 1986.

Willet, Andrew. *Hexapla.* Cambridge: Cantrell Legge, 1620. Accessed April 30, 2015. http://rarebooks.dts.edu/viewbook.aspx?bookid=1423.

Special Thanks

To my mom and dad – *Peggy* and *Jim Clifford*. Thank you for the sacrifice to send your seven children to Catholic schools. It was truly a gift and led me to my vocation as Catholic school teacher. Mom, thanks for your insistence when I was young that I read. Doing so helped me to become a bibliophile, therefore a more confident writer. Dad, your love for history and research has been a blessing to me. Thank you for all the insight that comes with that. Mom and Dad, I deeply appreciate the advice you gave me on this project. It really helps to have a mom who was an English teacher and a dad who was a journalist.

Father Tommy King – thank you for sharing your time and talent to help draw others closer to God.

Gary Meegan, Ed.D – thanks for the enthusiasm you showed for the project, kind words of support, and help reading the manuscript.

Brother Larry Scrivani, S.M. – your passion for and knowledge of Serra is, in my estimation, bar none. Thanks for your insight and direction with my research.

Patrick Vallez-Kelly, M.L.I.S. – I appreciate your invaluable help in tracking down resources through the years.

About the Author

Christian Clifford began teaching in the Archdiocese of San Francisco in 1996. He received his B.A. (Social Science) from the University of Great Falls, Montana, M.A. (Catholic School Teaching with an emphasis in Religious Education) from the University of San Francisco, Institute for Catholic Educational Leadership, and holds a California teaching credential.

Praise

Christian Clifford has captured the life and times of Fray Junipero Serra, The Apostle (soon to be Saint) of California. The book presents the humble and determined missionary's vision, historical accomplishments and work with the Native Americans in a clear and personal way. This book is a must-read for high school students in California's Catholic schools.

Kathleen H. Aikenhead, President, William H. Hannon Foundation, Santa Monica, California

Clifford has written a deeply personal and moving account of his search for the real Junípero Serra, a search rooted in primary sources. Responding to the intense questioning and challenges generated by the announcement of Serra's canonization by Pope Francis, Clifford pleads for a rational, empathetic understanding of Serra. Many modern critics will find the book disconcerting. Read this sympathetic study and make up your own mind.

Jeffrey Burns, Ph.D., Retired Archivist, Archdiocese of San Francisco

I found it an easy read and appreciated how well Christian Clifford synthesized complex issues that are both emotional and pertinent to understand why some would question and others be jubilant about Pope

Francis' announcement to canonize Fray Junipero Serra a saint in the Catholic Church.

Furthermore, Clifford enables the reader to utilize critical thinking skills based on well documented information and presents it in a concise work.

My background is 30 years of Catholic secondary education with twenty years as principal and president. In my view, his book will serve Catholic students well in courses like California History, American History as well as in Church History. Also, I encourage Mission gift shops to carry the book.

Rev. Thomas J. Elewaut, V.F., Pastor, San Buenaventura Mission, Ventura, California

We advocates of Junípero Serra's earthly works have long awaited and fervently prayed for the canonization of this holy man.

Since his veneration more than two centuries ago, much has been written about Serra. Christian Clifford offers a 21st-century perspective based on his research and devotion. Clifford's treatise, *Saint Junípero Serra: Making Sense of the History and Legacy,* is a keepsake as we celebrate Serra's sainthood in September 2015.

Terry Ruscin, Author, Columnist, Photographer, Former editor, *¡Siempre Adelante!*

Made in the USA
Charleston, SC
12 August 2015